The Complete Guide ,
in Secondary Educatioı

D1394485

Also available from Continuum

101 Essential Lists for Teaching Assistants, Louise Burnham
How to be a Successful Teaching Assistant, Jill Morgan
Teaching Assistant's Guide to Literacy, Susan Elkin
Teaching Assistant's Guide to Numeracy, Sara Fielder
Teaching Assistant's Guide to Autistic Spectrum Disorders,
   Jill Morgan and Ann Cartwright
Teaching Assistant's Guide to Dyslexia, Gavin Reid and
   Shannon Green
Teaching Assistant's Guide to Dyspraxia, Geoff Brookes
Teaching Assistant's Guide to ADHD, Kate Spohrer
Teaching Assistant's Guide to Emotional and Behavioural
   Difficulties, Kate Spohrer
Teaching Assistant's Guide to Managing Behaviour, Jill Morgan

The Complete Guide for Teaching Assistants in Secondary Education

GEOFF BROOKES

continuum

Continuum International Publishing Group
The Tower Building   80 Maiden Lane, Suite 704
11 York Road   New York, NY 10038
London SE1 7NX

www.continuumbooks.com

British Library Cataloguing-in-Publication Data
A catalogue record for this book is available from the British Library.

ISBN: 9780826499066 (paperback)

Library of Congress Cataloguing-in-Publication Data

Brookes, Geoff.
    The Complete guide for teaching assistants in secondary education / Geoff Brookes.
       p. cm.
    ISBN-13: 978–0–8264–9906–6 (pbk.)
    ISBN-10: 0–8264–9906–6 (pbk.)
    1. Teachers' assistants—Great Britain. 2. Teachers' assistants—Vocational guidance—Great Britain. 3. Education, Secondary—Great Britain. I. Title.

    LB2844.1.A8B68 2008
    373.114'1240941—dc22

                                                    2007038287

Typeset by Servis Filmsetting Ltd, Manchester
Printed and bound in Great Britain by MPG Books Ltd, Bodmin, Cornwall.

Contents

Introduction

Schools are all I know. I went from school to university and then back to school. I have been a teacher now for 34 years. You might think this amounts to very limited experience. You might think that I know little of life. You might think that my frame of reference is very restricted. There is so much that has not formed part of my life. I have had security of employment, a strong pension scheme. The trials of the free market, with its high risks and high rewards, have not been mine. It has been a comfortable time, spent largely with children, where relationships and authority are clearly defined. I have enjoyed it and it has suited me; it has kept my mind active and I have met a huge number of fascinating people. Oh yes, my professional life has had its limitations. And generally they rarely trouble me. But what it does mean is that I know what happens in secondary schools. They have been my life. Everyday I have gone to school and been a part of the things that schools do. I have had different roles during my career and I have taught in different kinds of places. If I know anything at all it is about how secondary schools operate and what it is like to be in one.

I have seen many changes in my career. Education is a world that never stands still and the rate of change has been particularly rapid in recent years. The teaching profession has been restructured and is being refocused. It is as a consequence of this that the job of teaching assistant was developed. It is part of the new world of education which has changed the way that teachers operate.

The role is not one that teachers have readily understood. But the benefits of teaching assistants are obvious and their role has been gradually embraced everywhere. And the reason why it has been accepted in many schools is the difference it makes in the classroom. Teachers are practical people. They like anything that makes their job easier and more successful and that is precisely what a good teaching assistant does.

The role that you will play is a vital one. You will influence achievement and well-being. Your support should make your students feel better about themselves, increase their confidence and ultimately improve their life chances, both socially and economically. The driving force behind the creation of such posts recognizes the great influence you are expected to have. Don't ever regard yourself as less important than a teacher. You are equally as effective in fulfilling the needs of the students; you do it with a teacher and perhaps in a different way. But you are fundamentally an integral part of the team that seeks out improvement and promotes learning.

You will need to have a grasp of the basics of child development, and an understanding of how to react to student behaviour. You will need to believe in the purposes of the school and support its processes. But most of all you will need to have a complete understanding of what a secondary school is like and what it is trying to do through its complex organization. This book is designed to be a guide to these unique and fascinating institutions.

1

What is it about schools?

Increasingly there is a sense that the government is keen to take greater control and direction of schools because they realize what a huge influence schools can have upon the shape of our future society. They do not want schools acting in an unstructured or maverick way. They have to go with the programme that has been established. Schools cannot stand outside a national agenda. So they have to promote health and the well-being of students and staff through the curriculum, they have to promote citizenship, they need to promote accessibility. Everything has to focus upon reducing inequalities. This concept of inclusion will play a major part in your professional life. And after a while, when you have started to understand what happens in schools, you begin to realize that they play a huge part in the national political arena.

Everyone has an opinion about them; everyone knows what should be done to make them a better place. They are under constant scrutiny and criticism. Teachers are told repeatedly that they can learn so much from the great captains of industry. The great excitement and cutting-edge innovation of the free market will teach schools greater efficiency and focus.

Yet your own experience will show you that schools are places of staggering complexity and that such simplistic assessments are rubbish. Schools are unique places. Indeed, industry and business have perhaps even more to learn from schools, certainly in the way we manage individuals and conflict. Schools should never be regarded as some sort of second-rate place.

Schools are criticized constantly about standards, but from what sort of perspective? Everyone has an opinion because they went to one, but does success in another field like business or industry make anyone better qualified to pass judgement? Does it somehow make their opinions more worthwhile than those of Mr Jones the milkman? Are his opinions more valid than those of the headteacher?

'Standards are falling, children are leaving school unable to . . .' Well, what is it this time? Read? Do simple division?

'They don't have the skills to . . .'

But what they are talking about is only part of the story. An important part, but not all of it. Schools reflect the society that they serve, and their function isn't only to prepare children for the world of work.

When I started teaching we were preparing for a world of leisure. Progress would free us all from drudgery. Machines would do it all. How wrong we were. Now everything is about preparing for employment, about maintaining our economic competitiveness. But if schools are only about work, then they will become dull and unsuccessful places.

We all must educate the whole person. And each whole person needs something different. For some they need to be part of the group, of the class and that is how they will progress through the system. Others will need far more individual support and help. To make sure the teaching works properly they will need an assistant who can provide effective interventions. The provision of an assistant such as yourself is a response to the richness of the student population.

What we should never do is to reduce education to mere training. We have no responsibility to create another cog in the wheel, a dutiful employee. Obviously this is far too simplistic, but never lose sight of the fact that school is part of what prepares students for life. Work will be an important part, just as it is for you, but it should only ever be a part. There are far more important things, like being a well-balanced and supportive member of society. To do that we need children who can think and ask questions and not merely accept what they are offered. We need dynamism and analysis, not acceptance. A good example of this is the system itself. Each generation changes the education system to show that their ideas are better than those that went before. So the system itself is in a constant state of flux. No one is ever satisfied. The system must always reflect a changing world.

So we can't have it both ways.

The world is either the same or it is not. When the world changes, so must education. And as society changes – the digital explosion, the new technology, new threats – so our schools will change to reflect this. They have to, because the world for which we are preparing our children is the one that we have created for them and they have to use it and adapt it for the sake of their own children.

You have a vital part to play in all of this.

The structure and the framework of schools are always changing. Education is after all an important element in the political arena. It is inevitable. New developments occur constantly in education. The concept of the extended school is one that may impact upon us all. This is a school that provides a range of activities and services to all members of the community and often beyond the school day. These services might include community sports programmes and adult education courses. A new idea, with extensive implications. As you can see, schools are places where the future is shaped. So if you want to shape society in a certain way, then you will take an interest in the nature of schools and think about what you want them to do.

There is certainly a belief that a life spent in schools is somehow inadequate. There are frequent calls made for teachers to find out about the 'real world', as if in some way ours is not. We have to find out about the health service, or business, or commerce. The implication always is that we must find out how to do things properly.

When people are sent into schools then it is always with the sense that education is too important to be left to the teachers.

But schools are not inadequate and you will see it for yourself.

You might bring different experiences yourself to the school. What you will probably see is that schools might do things differently but that is because they are very different kinds of places. They are not businesses, they are schools. They don't exist to make profits or to meet neat and uncomplicated targets. They teach children and it's a highly complex procedure. It can be messy and its progress isn't always easily distinguished. But they are not like other places.

Schools are confusing and wildly unpredictable. An industry has grown up of people who want to order and measure them and predict outcomes.

It is not possible. A school has a large number of people in it, drawn randomly from the community and beyond. They all have different needs and expectations and they are thrown together, with their different emotions and desires and they interact in an unpredictable manner in constantly changing circumstances. This makes schools infinitely interesting because they are never predictable. It makes schools very frustrating for those who believe they can be reduced to simple predictable outcomes. But in school every day is different.

The thought that you need to carry at the front of your mind always, is the name of your job. You are a teaching assistant and this puts you right at the heart of the school. Schools serve many purposes in a community. To some it is a child-care facility, to others it is an employment opportunity or a community centre. It gives teachers a job. It is a place for parents to meet and gossip. But of course, the most important purpose it serves is education and that is what frames your job.

What happens is that by bringing all these people together in different ways we prepare the future. It might sound pretentious, but that is why schools are so important. They shape the direction of our society. We shape minds and personalities. We influence lives. As a result of experiences, our young people often make choices about what they will do. They might wish to emulate a teacher they admire, to build upon a stimulating experience. A whole new world opens up for them.

That is what happens in schools, especially secondary schools, and that's why they are such special and important places. Lives are truly changed.

Teachers like any other professionals can, in the course of their work, drift away from an understanding of their core purpose. For many it becomes their job, rather than their career and they get sucked in to workplace misery.

But no other job has such far-reaching consequences and to be a part of it all is often a privilege.

Don't forget. You will make your own unique contribution to the mix. Think about it for a moment. Let us imagine that it is your job to support Kylie.

Last week Kylie had an argument with her PE teacher. You were able to talk to Kylie and calm her down, thus preventing Kylie from being excluded from school. This week however Kylie was given a detention for not doing her French homework, even though you reminded her. So she was pretty ratty by the time she got to PE. There was another row. This time you were delayed on the way to the lesson by a child who was sick in the corridor. By the time you arrived, you were unable to calm her down. She gets herself into a proper tizzy and swears at the teacher and at you. Suddenly and unexpectedly there was an issue.

This is just a simple example. The reality can be much more intricate. In any school on any day hundreds of individuals, most of who are in a completely different mood from yesterday, interact in a random manner. The consequences of this are completely unpredictable. No two classes are alike. No two days are alike. No two schools are alike. If you want a job that is nice and predictable then for goodness sake don't come anywhere near a school.

The fact that they operate at all is a triumph because they have astonishing complexity. And it's hard for those of us involved in education to accept the criticisms and crackpot ideas of those who have never been there and done it.

But everyone has an opinion about schools. They've been there, done it, saved the tie. So they know precisely what is wrong. We need to restructure the system to guarantee achievement.

So we have many different types of schools that change from generation to generation. Grammar schools, comprehensive schools, Academies, Foundation schools. Every few years we have a brand new idea.

But there are no simple solutions and the fundamental element of a school remains unchanged. It has always been the same wherever you go.

You put a bunch of kids together in a room and an older person tries to teach them something.

Sometimes it works; sometimes it doesn't. But we have to keep finding ways of making it successful.

There is a fundamental issue here – we gather children together as an economic means of delivering the knowledge we want them to acquire. However, we know that it is often the case that children learn best and indeed develop a skill if they are taught alone. I will not be the last teacher who has found a private maths tutor to help my children in an important subject that they were finding difficult. It was the only way to do it. Your job as a teaching assistant is very much in the same context as a private tutor. You are offering individual support as an informed intermediary between a student and the work they have been given.

It is all part of the way a school tries to make the impossible work and sometimes they succeed. But the basic experience doesn't change and schools look at different ways of managing it. What schools do is try to make this experience a successful one. It gives support and it structures the classroom experience, it identifies the different needs of individual learners. And that's where your job comes from. You can't treat a class of children as a nest of termites, small parts of one intelligence. They all want and need different things. And all those needs have an equal right to be fulfilled.

2

Applications and qualifications

Applying for a post as a teaching assistant is not something that you will do on a whim. It is something that comes at the end of a long period of reflection. It is a huge commitment to make – and indeed may represent a significant career shift.

It won't be the money that has attracted you either. There will be something within you that suggests that you are capable of making a difference.

You will want to make an emotional and professional investment in the future of our society. I know that it sounds pompous but that is what it is. You are expressing a desire to go off to school where you will work with the next generation and you will want to help them. You will have recognized just how important and influential learning should be. You will realize how disenfranchised young people can become if they do not engage with the learning process. This can have terrible consequences for the individual and for the shape of all our futures. You will have been through all these things inside your head. You can find posts as a teaching assistant by responding to advertisements, usually in the local press or online on various message boards or with teaching agencies. There is a website that maintains an up-to-date list of them (www.teaching-assistants.co.uk). You can consult national publications like the *TES*, the *Guardian* or the *Independent*.

You could also write to the local education authority and sometimes it is very effective to contact schools directly. Your letter might be the answer to someone's prayer.

But however much you like filing and sorting papers into a fascinating order and organizing piles of books neatly, you will never achieve anything in your job unless you are comfortable in the presence of children. Children and their needs are the key to your appointment.

There is a sense of comfort to some extent about working in schools. For many of us it is a return to a familiar world that we can recognize easily, especially for those of us who were achievers at school ourselves or were happy there. It can be an opportunity to recreate that comfort and security. For many it is less threatening than the cut-throat world of business or commerce or the tedium of being a small part of a huge bureaucracy. At least that is what my teaching assistants tell me. But going back to school is never the same. It can't be. Schools are different because they reflect the ways in which society changes. Think for a moment about all these new things that were never a part of your school days – mobile phones, internet chat rooms, cyber bullying. By the time you are reading this there is likely to be something else new that is exercising the concern of schools.

But the other thing of course is that your position will be different. Being an adult in school is very different from being a learner. You mustn't think that it is going to be the same.

In my own school we have employed a number of ex-students in different roles – some indeed as teaching assistants – and they find it a terrific shock and a huge adjustment largely because they see things differently now, with a wider perspective and with greater discrimination. Teachers they once admired are now seen as sadly fallible, their once-hilarious jokes having little currency in an adult world. Observing in the classroom is a very different experience from absorbing. So my ex-students bring to it a completely new perspective. They have changed and grown. Their ageing teachers had not.

But you will have to deal with these things yourself and you must be prepared for it. In fact it might not be a good thing to go back to the school that you left. Some people do of course, but I do think you need a newer and fresher view. You are never going to recreate your school days.

But you have made the decision now. What is your view of the job? Is it a stepping stone to something else? Is it a way of discovering whether you want to teach? There is nothing wrong with that at all. It is in fact a good move for some, since it enables you to achieve a greater knowledge and understanding, and indeed move on from your memories of your childhood.

Or is the job an end in itself? A decision to work with individual children rather than with classes of the little beasts? There is nothing wrong with that either. It is a noble decision that should be respected.

Again, you will need to ensure that you have a thick enough skin. Schools are not places for the hyper-sensitive. Like most that go to work in schools, you will have to change to survive. But you will be prepared to adapt because you will want to succeed.

Whether you are dipping your toe in the water or diving full length into the deep end, there must be a match between yourself and the school. You have to fit in – both with the aspirations of the school and the needs of individual learners. You would, for example, find it very difficult to promote the ideals of a high-achieving public school if you were convinced that capitalism should be overthrown by the fire-bombing of leading financial institutions. You do need to like the place where you work, especially if you are building a career. You need to like the work and like the place.

So clearly you need to carry out your research very carefully before you make an application. Send for the details of the school and look at them carefully. And of course, make sure you are sufficiently well qualified.

The phrase that is used about the necessity of proper qualifications, especially in English and maths, is a superb example of the way in which we use language today. On the government's own website (www.tda.gov.uk) it says that it is important for staff working in classrooms 'to feel confident about their own literacy and numeracy levels'. In other words, don't end up looking like a fool. Give off an aura of expertise. And it is a very good point. You need to know enough to be a few steps ahead of the students. It also says that 'Level 2 qualifications are essential for career progression'. That is clearly true, but they are essential for credibility too.

Children do not always discriminate between the different adults in schools. As far as they are concerned, we are all teachers. So we all need to display the commitment and knowledge of teachers. So always watch things like spelling and simple arithmetic. You will be expected to get them right.

I have interviewed candidates for teaching assistant posts and they have responded to the question about experience of working with children by telling me that they've got kids of their own. This might be relevant but only up to a point.

The sort of response a school might be looking for should be a bit more structured. Youth work, play schemes, nursery work, child care – all these are good examples of relevant experience. Other people's children are always the ones that will challenge you.

No one expects you to be the finished article. You may show that you have such potential, that previous experience is less significant than the other qualities you reveal. Whatever your background, there can be no expectation that you can walk straight into the school and be an effective member of staff right from day one. You will need to be prepared.

No one could expect you to deal with the complexities of school without training and the school should take a lead in ensuring that your skills are maintained and updated. Your appointment should also trigger LEA induction training.

But you will want to do your job properly and well, because this will give you pleasure. You will want to become a fully informed and effectively trained member of staff. There will be plenty of opportunities to do so and you should seize them. After all, schools are consumed by staff development. It is such a huge priority. Education is a fast-moving world and schools demand training opportunities. There are always new teaching schemes, new examination requirements, new equipment to be mastered. Teachers will try to keep up in their own time but there are many benefits to be gained from attending a course with other assistants. You will be able to exchange ideas and experiences.

Important opportunities for career development will be offered within school too. Suitable arrangements for appraisal will be established for you. This is a review of your performance conducted by you and your line manager. During the course of it you will review the targets that were set at the last appraisal, set new ones and identify any training or other help you might require. It should be a positive and an encouraging experience. It is an excellent way of thinking about your professional development and identifying your needs.

Prior to the meeting you may be asked to complete a self-review document in anticipation. This is a chance to think about the things that have happened to you and to think about where you might have been more effective. You will be able to talk about the things you have found interesting and would like to pursue and those things you have found less fulfilling. It could be the opportunity to examine your job description in the light of your experience.

It would also be very useful for all the teaching assistants in the school to hold regular meetings to discuss issues of common concern. Teachers do this; so should you. You should also attend full staff meetings and whole-school training events. You are, after all, part of the whole staff and no one should tell you any different.

You should always be looking for training opportunities because they keep your mind fresh and alert and give you a valuable opportunity to reflect on what you have been doing.

But working in school isn't like office work. The work cannot be piled up until you are back at your desk. Someone else has to take it over, either another colleague in an otherwise free lesson or more likely a temporary member of staff brought in to allow you to attend. And in these circumstances it costs the school money to ensure the opportunity is there for you. So you have an obligation to do your very best to make sure the training is worthwhile and effective. There will be people in school like a head of department or your mentor who can advise you about the training you need to find and to whom you can report back.

There are many opportunities for you within a career development framework for teaching assistants that has been produced by the Training and Development Agency for Schools which you can access on their website (www. tda.gov.uk). Here you will also find the national occupational standards for teaching assistants. These describe the activities you need to be able to carry out in order to be effective. It is very important that you are fully acquainted with them.

You will certainly need to develop study skills and there will be people in the school who will be able to help you with this. After all, schools are supposed to promote this and encourage independent learning. In this sense you are no different from the students you assist.

A school should appoint a mentor for each newly appointed TA who can give a whole-school perspective and induct you into what is a very complex organization, with its own history, politics and priorities. It is vital to give you the sort of focused and informed support that you will need, and an existing member of staff is best placed to give you such a framework to your job.

This will be a very important relationship and regular dialogue will be essential if you are to benefit properly from it. In the first instance they will ensure your successful induction into the school.

You will need to establish a clear picture straightaway of what your school is about and your mentor will help you to do this. They can provide basic factual information that will be essential. You will need to know who is who, you will need to know about general staff guidance and policies. A map could be extremely important. You will need to know about where the resource areas are and what they provide.

- Is there a quiet study and preparation area for staff?
- How can you get any photocopying done for example? Does any request need to be approved or do you have your own code number? Whose money are you spending when you use it? This can be an enormous source of friction in a department.
- What is the position on internet access?
- When was the last time the school was inspected by either Ofsted or ESTYN? What did the report say?

Of course as your first term disappears quickly and you rapidly become some sort of old lag, your relationship with your mentor will change. Your meetings will have a professional focus that is designed to support your career progression.

- Your meetings should provide the support you need, and an opportunity to sound off, to express your anxieties.
- They will help you structure your work and give you a chance to reflect on what you have seen.
- They will explain any issues or situations that might arise.
- They will put what you see into a wider educational context.
- The meetings will confirm the standards that the school expects.

- They will outline the priorities of the school.
- They will suggest professional networks that could help your personal development.

Of course, you will bring to the job a new and unique set of experiences – the things that have made you what you are. Whatever else you have done in your life will be valuable in the work you are to do, because life in a school must be enriched and informed by what happens in the wider world. So you should not be embarrassed by the things you have done. They have something in them that will help in your new job. You will have seen different things; indeed you will have had success and made mistakes. All these things go towards making you what you are and making you the sort of person that the school would like to appoint. A period of time as a window dresser? Not a problem. It shows you have an eye for arrangement and design. Work as a window cleaner? It shows you have a capacity for hard work and important experiences about health and safety for example that you can share with others. Nothing is irrelevant or worthless.

- So don't be ashamed of anything when you make your application.
- Of course, there is information that you will need about the school that will determine whether you will pursue your interest. How many students are on the roll? How many teachers work there? How many other TAs are there?
- Does the school have a special designation that might indicate it has certain priorities? Is it a church school for example?
- Is the school an Investor in People, meaning that it puts particular emphasis upon staff training?
- What sort of area does it serve? Is it rural or inner city?
- Does it have new communities or old estates?
- Do asylum seekers or refugees figure within the school?

- What are the employment opportunities like in the area?
- How is the school organized?
- How are the classes taught? Are the children taught in separate subjects right from the start of Year 7 or does the school have more of a cross-curricular emphasis?

Much of this you can find out either by talking to people or by looking on the internet. Most schools have their own website these days and they can be very informative, although the best source of information usually comes from the community who send their children there to be educated. What you need to do is to balance all these things up. Do your research properly and make a decision about whether or not you believe you will fit in and be able to make a contribution to the development and success of this community. It is informed candidates that schools want, not those who fire off applications for every possible job.

The structure of your job and the range of its responsibilities will be best served by pursuing further qualifications. Education is a fast-changing world and if you can't keep up you will not be able to do your job properly. You will probably want to progress because you will want to improve the way you do your job and it will certainly give you a framework against which you can assess the things you do. This could lead ultimately to career progression either in school as a teacher or indeed in some other role in children's services. Once you become integrated into the world of education then you will certainly find that there are indeed a huge number of interesting and rewarding career opportunities. Becoming a teaching assistant could be the first step in a life-changing progression.

Let us think for a moment about what skills you will need to possess.

You will need to be able to read and write. These are clearly essential skills. But your skills will be such that you will be able to reflect upon the work of others. You will need

17

to look at a child's work and offer corrections and improvements. And remember, a child will believe what you say and accept it as accurate. So you will need to ensure that it is.

- You will need to have a positive outlook – a genuine belief that you have something to achieve and that this job will be part of the way in which you can achieve your personal goals.
- The progress of children will be important to you and you will take pleasure in their achievement.
- You will be convinced that you can make a difference.
- You will also be comfortable in their presence. If you are not then you will find it difficult, if not impossible.
- You mustn't be easily offended. There will be occasions when the classroom and the staffroom will lack a certain sophistication and you will just have to come to terms with it. Remember that you will be working with children and they can be difficult and lack social skills.
- It is important that you have patience. The changes and the influence that you hope to have will not be achieved overnight. It takes time. The changes you effect will be gradual and there will be many false dawns and depressing setbacks.

Any adult has to be ready to become a role model to the children in school, and it is not something that you can command and control. The children make their selections and you cannot tell when it will happen. So you have to set a good example as much as you can. Things like picking up the litter or holding doors open must be second nature. In that sense there is never much time to relax. The old issue, which, thank goodness, isn't an issue anymore, is smoking. In the past it was difficult for adults in school to preach about smoking when they were doing it themselves. Children are no longer ready to accept the old arguments that adults are different and have more privileges. If they are not allowed to use a mobile phone in school then they will not be able to understand if you flaunt and use yours.

It is all about accepting responsibility when you work in school and remembering that you cannot escape from such expectations as the children have. You are in school and as a result you will forever be under their scrutiny. Any adult in school is, in their eyes, a teacher. You can't escape from it, so deal with it.

It is a surprise to some when they first come to work in a school. New employees in the school office are shocked when they realize that they are regarded by the students as an equivalent to a teacher. Children do not respond to a job description; they respond to the age of the person and their presence. They expect you to show these qualities and they do not give you any time to acquire them. You have a level of responsibility from the moment you enter the building. It is inescapable. You have to be ready and willing to play the role that is expected of you.

3

What is the job of a teaching assistant?

You will find yourself working during school hours and often only during term time, but this makes employment opportunities very flexible. It is possible to fit in an effective job as a teaching assistant with child-care obligations with some gentle adjustments, just as long as what you can offer fits in broadly with what the school needs. You will need to be in school on those occasions when the children you are supporting will be there. You will be able to do some work when they are not in school but largely the work you will do will be in supporting the students in their learning.

There are generally four different types of support that a teaching assistant gives – and this sort of support is the essential element of your job.

You will be expected to provide:

- Support with classroom resources
- Support with caring for learners
- Supporting learning activities
- Supporting colleagues

These different areas are not separate; they are interdependent. You will offer different kinds of support at different times.

21

One of the first things you must do is to become familiar with the school's documentation. This is a vital step. Through it you will learn about the approach to inclusion, the examinations policy, attitudes towards behaviour. You will learn about the sort of priorities the school has, where it puts its emphasis and perhaps resources.

It will tell you everything that you need to know about your school. It will reveal its particular identity and you will be expected to adopt it.

The documentation will also contain details of all policies. How behaviour is dealt with, the way the assessment and reporting system operates, how bullying is dealt with. Never think that these are just meaningless documents. They are not. They are a guide showing you how to react and the details in them will protect you. In any circumstance, you need to show that you have acted in accordance with the established school policy, which in turn will have evolved out of some other document, possibly with legal standing. Thus your protection should always be that you followed procedures. It is when you depart from procedures that problems often occur.

You will work with individual children, small groups and even perhaps on occasion, with a whole class, particularly if you chose to qualify as a Higher Level Teaching Assistant. This will bring increased responsibility as well as an increased salary.

Of course you are unlikely to be alone. Most teaching assistants in a secondary school are part of a team and work from a base within the learning advice, learning support or special needs department. This will become a very important feature of your work. You will become a part of a department and share with their hopes and achievements. You will build important friendships there from which you will learn a great deal and it is where you will always find the support of your colleagues.

'Assistant' means someone who helps or supports. That is exactly what you will be doing. You will be offering support.

First of all, and most importantly, you will be helping the learner. Your title is 'teaching' assistant, not 'teachers' assistant, which is an important distinction. The help you offer will take many different forms. At one level you might be attending to their private and personal needs, depending, of course, on the students themselves. At another level, and perhaps this is less obvious, you will be promoting and encouraging inclusion and acceptance. You will support them and in so doing add to their confidence, showing them that they can be successful and popular members of society. Isolation from and neglect by their peers will not help their personal growth. Constructive relationships initiated by you could have a huge influence on a child's development. Everything else that you do will have far less importance.

Of course you will support the teacher in many ways, both as part of your job and because you are a friendly adult in the classroom. Your work will involve the practicalities of teaching and learning. Teaching assistants do many things and this can make the job varied and interesting. It is certainly unpredictable, switching from the mundane to the unusual in minutes. The job will also draw upon skills that are founded within your own maturity. So you might be offering assistance to children in how to hold a pen or to fasten shoelaces. You might be playing educational games or reading. You could be taking notes in lessons to act as a reminder, supporting a child while they manage their work. You could be doing something as mundane as carrying a bag and some books around school. You are there to support and facilitate learning, to enhance teaching.

You will have some idea of what you will be expected to do from the job description you will be given on your appointment. It might indicate work with a particular student or it could have more general aspects but it shouldn't prevent you from becoming a fully committed professional. So you might also assist with tidying up or displaying work. You might keep records, especially recording information about your particular student. But it is inevitable too that you will be involved in maintaining good order in the classroom. You cannot and must not avoid this responsibility. If there's a problem, then get stuck in. Your personal credibility will disappear if you sit back and refuse to engage. 'But it's not my problem . . .' Well quite frankly, it is. Because in the kids' eyes you will be regarded as impotent, an adult sanctioning and embracing chaos. So you have to respond, even if all you can do is to alert someone else to the emergence of a problem.

It is a role that does not begin and end in the classroom. Your relationship with students will be such that you need to support them at all times and certainly if events seem to be developing in a corridor or a dining hall, you have an obligation to intervene. You can never walk past on the other side. What you will therefore be showing is that there is a continuum of good behaviour that encompasses all aspects of the school. It is not something that can be switched on and off on different occasions. You will be teaching moral and consistent behaviour within the school community.

You will help to manage behaviour successfully in the classroom by working with teachers. It will always be a team approach. You will work together to prevent issues arising through measured intervention and planning. You can talk about seating plans for example. You will talk about the nature of the lesson and so you will be able to predict possible issues and develop individual resources. In these ways the status of the teaching assistant will be enhanced.

It is a good job that you should enjoy and it has opportunities for professional development and advancement. You can progress to become a Higher Level Teaching Assistant and then to become a qualified teacher. These stages are outside the scope of this book but you will be doing the school and yourself a disservice if you settle permanently into a specific role and do little to progress it. You must never stagnate. Schools always move on – and so should you.

The qualifications required will vary from school to school. Many are looking for older applicants with wider life experiences. There are always elements in the work that draw upon caring skills. Thus an age differential between a teaching assistant and the children will be seen as desirable. However, other schools take a different view and are keen to appoint younger candidates with a more recent experience of education and more empathy perhaps with learners. Perhaps their own successes and failures ensure that they can act as impressive and more immediate role models. So much depends upon the nature of the school and what it perceives as its requirements at a particular time or with a particular student.

Obviously a qualification in English and maths is very important, since these are two areas where you might be spending part of your time. You can't expect to maintain your credibility with either students or staff if you cannot complete simple maths without a calculator.

There are training courses and specific qualifications available but at present (2007) they are not regarded as essential. It isn't impossible however to envisage a time when certificates or apprenticeships are mandatory.

But when you consider the job, what is it that a school expects from the person whom they appoint?

- The first and foremost expectation that you will need to fulfil is that you will support the institution. This means that you have to want the school to succeed. If the school means nothing to you, then go somewhere else. Working in a school is always more than a job.
- One of your obligations is to keep yourself informed. You could get yourself into terrible trouble if you acted inappropriately, without the awareness of changing legislation or policies. So be aware of all child protection policies and procedures. Ignorance is never any kind of defence.
- You must value the students you work with and support. Listen to what they say and take pride in their achievements. That doesn't mean to say that you need to be a soft touch. Be firm and realistic but don't lose your sympathy.

- Don't overreact to what children say. Never forget that they are children and that they have a right to make mistakes. Correcting students who let a swear word slip and looking disappointed is much more effective in the long run than marching them off for summary execution. You need to keep a balance. That's what the school wants; a sense of perspective.
- You will need to show initiative if you are going to succeed. Deal with minor issues as a responsible adult should in a school.
- Maintain a sense of proportion – and realize when you are out of your depth. If you are in doubt about anything that has happened then you must refer it on straightaway. It is better that way.
- You need to be confident about your own literacy and numeracy skills. It is certainly an important area for career progression and, of course, you will be leading your students in these areas. You are there to set an example and to offer appropriate advice and support.
- You will need to make a contribution to maintaining order in the school. If you walk past problems because you say that they are not your responsibility, then you are not the sort of appointment the school needs.

Supporting the school is something that eventually should become second nature.

Once appointed, you will become part of the school and you will find yourself identifying with it very quickly. Don't be surprised if it takes over a part of your life. That's what schools do. As you become a member of staff you will absorb the priorities and the history of the place.

You will drift into the gossip, listening to it with understanding and contributing towards it. You will want the place to succeed.

If the first place you work doesn't do this for you, then you will move on to another school where you will suddenly feel at home. It is what happens. The realization will be that you care about this untidy and possibly inefficient building and the people who work in it. You will want to protect its reputation and be proud of what it does. You will be pleased when the students stop and speak to you when you are shopping. You will want to be part of everything that goes on.

Schools are complex communities in which many different things happen. The school Christmas concert or the annual drama production take up a huge amount of time. The very best of these events draw upon the help and enthusiasm of many different staff across the school. Everyone can find a role to fulfil – whether it be lights, make-up, supervising the cast backstage. They are often truly wonderful occasions where the excitement of the children is infectious and moving. You really should get involved, if at all possible. It will introduce you to a wide range of pupils whom you wouldn't otherwise meet and it will cement your place in the school. There is nothing better than that happy smile you'll get from a cast member when you walk past them in the corridor. And always ask about exam results and achievement. In this way you are reinforcing the priorities of the school.

Your example should encourage the children you work with to get involved too and they will have unrivalled opportunity to be part of the school community that they often do not have the self-confidence to join. The benefits in terms of developing their confidence and their self-esteem are enormous. It is another example of how you can become an influential role model.

Sporting events are important opportunities too. You gain credibility through your support, because you are a person who cares. Ask about who played well, who made a vital intervention. It is tremendously important if the child you support plays for the team. Take an interest. Ask them to write you a report or give you a verbal impression of what happened. Or better still, you can turn up and write a report yourself to be read in assembly. It is something the team will always remember and it is an investment that at sometime or other you will be able to draw on. It is all about building successful relationships which will help you in your role in the school. Not only that, but they will help the students you support in many ways. You won't be a sad old auntie or uncle who sharpens pencils for thick losers. You will be seen as an interesting and involved person who is doing a proper and worthwhile job. You can counter some possible negative publicity in this way.

It is the same for teachers too. No matter how good a teacher they are in the classroom, they still need to engage with the wider life of the school. Without such involvement, they will remain one-dimensional.

Schools are not just places where we go to earn money. They are communities to which we will eventually belong. It is what makes them such good places to work.

In the end though the classroom is one of the key arenas in which you will work. This is where you will become aware of the special nature of your job. Neither teacher nor student, you will operate in the space between them to ensure the success of learning. It is a unique position.

In the first place you will need to establish with any teacher you are with exactly what it is that is happening in the lesson so that you will know what you are looking for and so that you can judge whether or not it is successful.

You will be trying to provide reliable information on progress and so determine how the learning has been absorbed. The information you provide should inform the teacher and the learner and show what must happen next. So a teaching assistant should be able to make a judgement about how the student has been able to work independently and how well they have been able to work with others.

You should also question the learner gently to see whether they have understood the full implications of the lesson because this will inform the next stage and determine what, if anything, you need to do. Should you devise some simple questions to ask at a later date to show that they have grasped the issues? Or will you need to repeat the whole business with them on some other occasion outside the classroom, in a tutorial perhaps?

One of the main contributions you might make will be in differentiation. This is the means by which one piece of work is adapted so that it can be accessed by students of differing levels of ability. With the knowledge of your students that you will develop through sustained close contact, you will be well positioned to differentiate material, which can be achieved in a number of different ways.

- You can group students who are making progress at a similar rate by gathering them together at one table for example so that they can work together. They will help each other understand concepts since they will be able to work them out collaboratively. You will be able to help a range of learners by making a range of interventions. This will also shelter a child from embarrassment if they feel that they are not alone in asking for help.
- You can differentiate work for students by setting different tasks for students which have been designed with their particular abilities in mind. In its simplest form, this would involve designing simpler worksheets with different, less complicated tasks.
- A teacher can set tasks and then allow students to respond in their own way at different levels. This is called differentiation by outcome. It can be seen in a simple form in a creative writing assignment in English. Everyone might get the same title for their story but each student would respond in a different way that would reflect their ability.
- You can achieve differentiation by offering different levels of support.

The concept of differentiation is extremely effective in mixed-ability settings where students are grouped together merely on the basis of age rather than on any particular level of ability. This generally happens at Key Stage 3, though it does occur sometimes in option subjects at Key Stage 4.

Mixed ability does have significant benefits in that it helps students learn from each other and promotes a sense of inclusion. However, it does need careful and dedicated management by teachers and it doesn't always work in all subjects with all teachers. It can make huge demands upon staff to prepare accessible material in different ways. As a teaching assistant you will be expected to play a leading part in these preparations, and you are likely to find it a very enjoyable part of the job.

In some other situations the students are grouped together on their aptitude in a subject, with the intention of achieving success more rapidly and in a group of learners with similar understanding and needs. Of course, in such setting arrangements students may not always be in the same group. They could be in a higher set in English than they are in science for example.

Different arrangements may well operate in different parts of the school. What is important is that the progress of all students is what should determine how these things are organized. Whatever happens, you will be expected to provide support within the context that the teachers have established. For effective learning to take place there must always be effective teaching, and in some classrooms you will be an essential element in ensuring that this happens.

4

Relationships with students

You will be an intermediary between the two most important groups of people in the school, the teachers and the children. You are there to facilitate the success of relationships with both parties in order to ensure that learning takes place. So it is only right that we look in this chapter and the next at how you can work with two groups that can often seem rather idiosyncratic.

Let's start with the students.

You will need to establish high-quality relationships – professional and caring – with the children in the school. It is their school and it exists to serve their needs, not yours and not the teachers'. We should only ever do those things in school that enhance their education. So we should listen to them and determine the actions that will make the school a better place. But that certainly doesn't mean that we should be completely and uncritically child-centred. If you want to succeed you will need to deal with things professionally and with an adult perspective. Children get things wrong and we have to help them rectify mistakes and learn from them. As children, they have a right to make mistakes.

You are not a mate who forgives everything. You are a critical friend. You don't try to buy friendship by being soft and easily conned. It won't get you anywhere. Being soft isn't really caring. Caring can involve hard decisions. So you need to be able to say that 'because I want you to succeed, I can tell you that what you are doing is unacceptable'.

You need to be supportive, but there's more to it than being big brother or big sister. It is called 'tough love' and sometimes saying the hard things which hurt are the right and proper things to say. Confronting errors and mistakes is better than ignoring them.

To deal with specific issues like ADHD (attention deficit hyperactivity disorder) or other particular difficulties you might need specialist and focused training. But often in the day to day business of the classroom what you rely upon will be your experience and your maturity. If something is wrong then it is wrong and should be acknowledged, not ignored.

Current research tells us that for learning to take place most effectively the learner must be relaxed. If there is stress or anxiety then the blood moves away from the part of the brain used for thinking and towards the brain stem where instinctive responses are based. Stress and conflict can stop learning taking place. So an important part of your job is to build the sort of trusting atmosphere which will allow learning to happen. Keeping fear out of the learning environment should be one of your most important priorities.

Obviously there needs to be a sense of respect and that means giving students a right of reply. Always listen, and that, in fact, is one of the best things you can do. Be available and listen. If a student makes the effort to come and see an adult in school it is usually because they have something they need to say, so we should all be ready to listen to them. They might have a problem or they might be confused or they might have a little happiness to share. Listening carefully will develop trust and trust from one student will often grow to encompass others.

And whatever it is that you do, that trust will come from the students themselves. You cannot initiate it, except by being approachable and confident. They will always select the staff who are important to them. You can't select but you should think twice before you reject.

Never dismiss what they say to you out of hand, no matter how unlikely it might appear. They will have told you something because they trust you. Or because they are trying perhaps to manipulate you. We have to accept that this does happen. At some point you will need to make a judgement. You are an adult working in school who is not a teacher. They may have bad feelings about teachers as a result of too many bad experiences, too many times reminded of their failures. But they may need to talk to someone who they think can help, and that person might indeed be you.

This puts you in a position of particular strength and influence. You will find out things that no one else knows. I don't mean by this that you should promote yourself as some kind of roving agony aunt. But focused work with an individual child can mean that unexpected disclosures are made. And then a whole machinery with which it is your duty to be acquainted will spring into action and take over.

You mustn't think that child abuse is happening everywhere but, on the other hand, you do need to be aware of some of the indicators of abuse. Certainly if you see any of these and are sufficiently concerned then you are failing in your responsibilities if you don't pass this information on. It may be nothing at all but if it is a problem then you would never forgive yourself for not speaking up when first you worried.

You should be alerted by:

- Unusual or troubled behaviour
- Bruises, injuries, marks
- A sudden withdrawal from normal activity
- Other signs of neglect, like dirty clothes

It is certainly not your responsibility to investigate allegations of abuse. But you need to listen carefully to anything you are told and pass that information on as a matter of urgency. There are trained people, including the police and social care workers, who have that responsibility. Don't feel that you have let anyone down or betrayed a trust when you pass these things on. You are carrying out your duty. You can never offer any child complete discretion. That is sometimes hard, but a fact of life. What would you want for your own child? It is always important to remember that you are in fact a role model. The students will watch you, especially those with whom you work most closely, and they need to see you maintaining your reactions to situations, remaining calm and polite and professional. If the school rule is that trainers cannot be worn, then don't wear yours to school. It makes the students feel angry about what they perceive as an injustice and an inconsistency. But of course you should always dress professionally anyway, so your trainers will never become an issue, will they?

In all this you are supporting students in a vital aspect of learning. You are helping them develop and grow as people and better equipping them for all the other things that are likely to happen in their lives. Many have arrested development in important areas and through the behaviours you model, you will be able to show them solutions and successes. They will be more capable of building lasting relationships and being responsible adults.

In behaviour management terms, raging and screaming at someone in the adult world rarely works. So we need to show a range of responses to situations within school as well. Of course there can be an issue if you don't hit it off with a student you have been allocated. This can be a real problem. You should expect to be working with some of our most troubled and frustrated students. They might indeed be unpleasant and obstructive, rude and dismissive. Of course we will say that it is your job to win them over, but I am afraid to say that this is not always possible. So you must try. Be patient. Be forgiving. You never know, your student may never have had an opportunity to learn how to be nice. Your continued good humour and support might be the key that unlocks a particular door. Huge changes might follow.

But they might not. And if, after all you have done, there is no progress at all, then it might be necessary to say that enough is enough. The student's interests of course are paramount and we have to accept that actually the problem might be you. A change of teaching assistant might be all that is needed. We have to accept that and move on. Don't take it personally and neither give nor receive any blame.

Be adult about it. We have to accept that this can happen. A new start can help in many other situations. Why not here?

If the child is using you, is trying to punish you for what has happened to them, then don't worry. It doesn't hurt. Work with the other teaching assistants and shuffle the pack, reallocate responsibilities.

It does become an adult-focused problem however, if you start to feel uncomfortable with a particular student. It might be because they exhibit behaviour by which you are troubled. You might feel threatened by what they say or might do; you might feel that you are unable to influence their behaviour to the extent that their health and safety is at risk. In which case therefore you must tell someone. It is not brave or heroic to sacrifice your own peace of mind. Change the dynamic as soon as possible. I know a teaching assistant who became a completely different employee once she had been released from the burden of working with a girl with epileptic fits who would frequently run away from school into the busy traffic. She found the strain enormous and an overdue reallocation of responsibilities changed her into a highly effective member of staff. A more experienced person, better prepared by life experiences, took over. Everyone was much happier. And all this happened because we were told. So always keep your manager informed and be prepared to be active rather than a passive victim.

Everyone has rights in school. No one person's rights are more important than anyone else's rights and in recent times increasing prominence has been given to the opinions of the students of the school. They have been more integrated into the management and the organization of the school.

It is seen as increasingly important that students are involved in the organization and running of the school. Giving the students a voice is vital. The school is a significant part of their life. They have excellent ideas, though they can be very assertive and lacking in subtlety. They see things very much in black and white and are, for example, very punitive. Not for them a measured balancing of the perpetrator's needs as well as the victim's. They are always ready to deal with their peers in a vigorous way! Forgiveness and compassion are there, but sometimes you need to look for them. Vengeance is mine, saith the Lord. I shall repay. Unless of course you are the school's council.

They take pride in their school and believe in the importance of it. They desire for it to do well and are always disappointed at any poor publicity it might receive. I have had to deal with students angry at some misrepresentation in the local press, desperate to write letters and speak to reporters to redress the balance. It is a reminder that however close we feel to the school as adults, it isn't our school. It is theirs.

Teachers can feel intimidated by them and feel on the whole that they have been given far too much power and influence. They are only children after all, is the general impression. Yet their involvement can bring enormous benefits.

A student council can make the fiercest of interview panels, asking the hardest questions and forming unshakeable opinions. They want the best teachers working in their school and are certainly not swayed by false attempts at seeking popularity.

They have a genuine concern for their environment and can often see improvements that will make a real difference that will actually pass by other, older, people.

The school's council is a symbol of how we take student opinions very seriously. The responsibility it brings can be a powerful tool for change. I have seen a minor villain in the school transformed by his election to the school council. His mates all got together and engineered Simon's election as a bit of a disruptive laugh. It backfired. He was completely committed to his work and changed his outlook on school entirely. Responsibility created a sense of responsibility. This is one of the most important functions that student councils serve. They make a positive contribution in improving relationships and reducing bullying and vandalism. All students should make an effort to become involved.

In your work as a teaching assistant you must support the work of the student council. Encourage those students you work with to find their own voice and to ensure that their views are represented. You may need to explain to them the purpose that it serves and why they should be involved. But the benefits they may derive could be considerable. They mustn't feel that the school council is for someone else. It should represent everyone, even those struggling, in difficulties or the disengaged.

As you can see, if you don't already know it, working with children can be great fun. It definitely keeps you on your toes.

5

Teachers

They are an odd bunch of people. I should know; I have spent my life with them. Interestingly, my wife has spent her life with just one teacher and she will often say that teachers are most peculiar. Odd how we have arrived at the same conclusion.

I would have to say that some of the most gifted and talented people you will ever meet will be teachers. Their frame of reference can be astonishing and their ability to make complicated concepts sound simple and obvious is a remarkable talent. If you think about your own education, then you will remember those jolly and exceptional people who made their lessons so interesting and successful. These people had an effect on you that has lasted for many years. They established an atmosphere for learning and inspiration that marks out a gifted teacher with the ability to touch lives.

But there are also a number of teachers who are just plain weird. The job can have a strange effect upon people. It certainly affects the way in which they see the world and the way they relate to the people around them. They cannot do their job unless they are in control and so they must maintain control at all times in their own little kingdom, the classroom. For them their entire career has been based upon conflict. When that classroom door closes they are in charge. Only they and the students know pre-cisely what has been going on, because when someone else is there to observe, things are entirely different. Teachers can view their working life as a constant war between good and evil, composed of a series of battles and skirmishes that they must always win. They feel that they are always tee-tering on the brink of chaos. What this means therefore is that they are not very good at following instructions. They feel that it is better to give them, rather than receive. In any circumstance they always know best.

This means that they are notoriously difficult to manage and it can make some of them very difficult to work with. They can be deeply conservative and reluctant to consider any changes or adaptations. They may have little time for managers or for innovation. They have seen it all before and it never worked the first time round. These will be class-rooms in which you won't like working too much. And probably many of the students won't like it much either. It will be too inflexible and tense. They might well regard a teaching assistant as an intruder and do little to integrate you into the business of the classroom. These can be diffi-cult circumstances, since you will need to use your initiative to plan work and to support the child without a great deal of guidance. It is not unusual for a teaching assistant to deal with repeated requests to carry out tasks like last-minute photocopying which are designed to get them out of the classroom. If this happens then it is an issue that you need to address with your line manager. However uncomfortable the teacher feels in having another adult in the room, this is not important. What matters is that the needs of the child are met. That is why you are there. The teacher's feelings are unimportant.

But while you may come across such a circumstance – and your teaching assistant colleagues will no doubt exchange stories about their own experiences in this class-room – it will not generally be the norm. Teachers are too practically minded to allow the opportunities that you present to pass them by. You will be seen as an answer to their prayers if you can provide workable solutions to classroom difficulties. The fact that you can help them by taking one or more children out of the classroom equation means that they can get round to see more children in the lesson. So they will be happy to work with you and provide you with details of what they are working on in the classroom. It is also true to say that they may welcome the fact that you keep them on their toes. Because you will be there, they will always ensure their lessons are planned and prepared.

It is always good to talk to teachers about their lessons and generally they will be pleased to do so. In this way you will learn a great deal. You will also find that new ideas will keep sparking off when you do start talking about professional issues.

Your perspective can give you an advantage over some of the teachers you will work with. It can be very difficult for a classroom teacher to achieve the same cross-curricular experience that your job gives you. They would have to seek out a professional development opportunity and ask for their lessons to be covered. This can be very useful since it shows them what is happening in different parts of the school but it is also expensive for the school. And yet this experience is yours as a part of your daily work. So you can tell them what is happening in other areas and they will be able to see opportunities to link their work together. This will definitely benefit the children.

It is always a good idea to check with a teacher what is actually going to happen in a lesson so that you can prepare yourself. This could be very important if your own skills are to be challenged. You don't want to look foolish for example in a practically based subject if you are having to confront something that you cannot do. This might well be the case in a PE lesson or in a technology subject. The problem is that you run the risk of looking stupid, and this could have a serious impact upon your credibility. Another example could be drama, a subject in which you might feel too self-conscious to make a suitable contribution. The child you support may well believe that you are in fact no better than they are. It might bring you together; on the other hand, it might drive you apart. So always make sure that the teacher prepares you for what might happen in a lesson. Apart from anything else, preparing resources is great fun and helps professional development.

What you will also find is that teachers teach in entirely different ways, even close friends who teach within the same subject. However much teaching is constrained and restricted in an attempt to give each child the same experience, it isn't possible. The personality of the teacher is a vital part of the classroom. Children respond to it; it makes learning happen – or sometimes prevents it from happening. But the teacher is what you pay for and they are by far and away the most expensive item in the classroom – and the most unpredictable.

Teachers get stressed because teaching is a performance. A lot of what we do in school isn't natural. And sometimes you don't feel like doing it. But the nature of school is such that you cannot pick or choose when that performance is to be put on for you are governed by an inflexible timetable. So it doesn't matter whether the class are not quite ready for a maths lesson. Or that a particular student would prefer to run around the field at that moment. No one has a choice, so everyone has to get on with it. It doesn't matter whether it is the right moment or not. A teacher can feel that they are barely holding the kids in check and can become tense or nervous because of some completely different issue, which can negatively affect their performance. Many different things can disrupt that performance.

It is also important to respect the efforts and the investment that teachers have made in engaging with their chosen subject. They have invested heavily in terms of training and intellectual time and space. When their lesson is condemned or rejected they can often feel that this is personal. That in fact they themselves are being rejected when their lesson is dismissed as boring or irrelevant. And that rejection hurts.

You will see this as you tour the school, observing lessons. You will understand how so many of them can approach their job with such a lack of confidence or why they never seem completely relaxed. This is why some lessons become all about control. The children must queue outside, they must stand behind chairs, they must wait for the word to sit down, the register is taken. It is a highly effective sequence for calming a class down, for getting them to focus upon the new lesson. It is a refocusing of attention. It brings their minds and attention back into line.

Other teachers do different things. Instead of calming them down they like to stir them up. They believe in the exciting nature of their subject, that the engagement and interest will encourage behaviour. They are not fearful of bad behaviour; on the contrary they expect good behaviour at all times and are disappointed when they don't get it. There is a lot to be said for this approach. Make it interesting, make it fun, make the children want to be there and they will learn.

As they move around the school all children become very skilled at dealing with these different styles and cope happily with the changing expectations made upon them. In fact they move around the school in a very sophisticated way, learning how teachers behave and responding accordingly. Both styles are effective in the hands of a practitioner who is skilled in using them and your position will enable you to reflect upon the way that teachers operate.

Naturally this can make your relationships with teachers very difficult because you will be in their classroom and they won't be able to avoid the feeling that you are watching closely and making judgements which at some later point will be passed on to someone else. Make no bones about it. They can find your presence very threatening. But of course the important thing – as in any relationship – is to communicate properly. As a teaching assistant you should always ask questions anyway to find out what is going on and to formulate your role in a particular lesson. The old idea of a teaching assistant, performing clerical and administrative tasks, has gone but a residual memory remains in the minds of some teachers. So always ask the teacher what they are doing and be willing to help them prepare the lesson, with an emphasis of course upon your own specific student. Ask them what their objectives are in the lesson. Think of ways that they may find useful within the context of their own teaching style. And never forget that your own position is very privileged since you see things across the school, so use that knowledge to suggest improvements. Most will be very pleased to listen to you and in such a way a proper working relationship will develop.

In the end you need to be an integral part of the planning and the organization. To be truly effective you should be able to exchange constructive feedback with the teacher as part of a team that shares a common goal in promoting learning and achievement. Some teachers will be very unhappy with this concept but many more will not and will see the exciting possibilities that your job presents. In the best lessons, the teaching assistant and the teacher will work as an integrated team, with no self-conscious division of labour. You can ensure that vulnerable students maintain concentration and engagement while the overall shape of the lesson is not compromised by distractions. This sort of involvement will help you to form your own overall career objectives.

So always concentrate upon the professional role that you have been asked to perform. You are not teacher's little helper. It is the role of the additional professional in the room that you need to adopt. And the purpose of what you do is always to improve learning and ultimately the life chances of the students you deal with.

6

Parents

Never dismiss the role of parents in the whole of the education process. They are a vital part of the whole. Many teachers do not engage with parents very regularly, yet in the course of your work you may well have far greater access than they would ever expect. Parents' consultation evenings may be the limit of their contact, and it might well be brief and rather superficial. Your contact may well be much more significant.

You will be dealing with children with particular needs and their parents will regard you as a walking symbol of the fact that their child needs additional help. They will value your attention. They are generally very grateful for what you do and are rather flattered and intrigued by the level of interest that your support implies. Your insights will be respected and acknowledged. They will want to know what you think of their child and the progress they are making. After all, you might actually spend more time with them than anyone else, including their parents, during a normal school week. They may well ask your advice about different issues, especially if the school feels the need to establish further provision for the child. They will ask you what you think. So you are in a privileged position and you will be expected to respond honestly and professionally. If their child has specific learning difficulties, then they will expect you to be able to offer some sort of insight about it. They themselves may know very little about the problem, whether it be Asperger syndrome or ADHD. But they will expect you to be able to speak about it knowledgeably. This is an important point. It is your responsibility to keep yourself fully informed of the implications of any condition that a child you support may carry. The parents are as likely to ask you about it as they are anyone else, so make sure that you have something sensible to say. Your first response when you are given a new student to support must be to find out as much as possible about them and their difficulties, so ask the learning advice department for a full picture. It is far more sensible to prepare for this and to look ahead than to appear foolish and ill-informed at a crucial moment.

You may also meet very well-informed parents. They will be aware that their child has an issue. They might feel very guilty about passing this problem on to the child they love and so they will do whatever they can to help them. They may have become very well informed about the one problem that their child might have, such as dyspraxia. This should indicate to you that you need to stay as informed as possible about any of the conditions that you are dealing with. You will look extremely foolish if the parents know more than you when they are looking to you and the school to provide workable solutions to the difficulties they are facing as a family. You will ask the people around you for advice but you will also listen to the parents. You will welcome the meetings you hold with them so that you can improve the overall provision that you can offer the student through greater understanding. Never dismiss the perspective that parents have. You will be surrounded by professionals with many impressive qualifications but the people who know the most about a child are in almost all circumstances the parents themselves. It is often the case that teachers speak quite dismissively of parents. They are regarded as an inconvenience, those tiresome individuals who ask tiresome questions. But we are in the jobs that we have in order to provide proper solutions to the difficulties with which these families are asked to wrestle. Do not forget either, that any parent has every right to complain if there is something that they are not happy about. They are no different to anyone else. You can complain if you receive poor service anywhere. So can they. In fact, in my experience, teachers are the very first to criticize other teachers who may not be teaching their children with the sort of attention that they think they deserve. And if it is good enough for them, then it is good enough for others too.

Everyone has the right to complain. Perhaps we need to remember that a difficult parent is perhaps just a caring one. Perhaps we all have the capacity to be difficult if we are sufficiently provoked. It is an important thing for you to keep at the front of your mind. In my experience one of the issues that can provoke the greatest anxiety among parents is bullying. Quite rightly, if they feel that their child is being physically intimidated then they will demand to be heard. This is a matter for the senior managers of the school to address, to make sure that the school has a coherent and realistic policy.

It remains a genuine concern in all schools, especially now that bullying has started to take on many new and unexpected forms as children use all the different forms of electronic communication. Awareness has grown and children are more inclined to seek help. Bullying is now the single biggest reason for distress calls to Childline. Is there more of it? Or is it that its profile has been raised and reporting has increased? The fact remains that schools need to deal with it.

Bullying is action that is designed with the sole purpose of being hurtful. It is never accidental. It is repeated and the victims find it hard to defend themselves from it.

Schools must have an approach that encompasses the whole of the community and confront it by bringing it out into the open. You have an important role to play in this.

Bullying survives in the dark, in the half-light. When it is brought out into the open it will wither and die. That is why it is so important for it to be revealed. Obviously you must never promise a child any level of confidentiality. You have to retain the possibility of passing on the information that you receive. You might feel the need to talk to a form tutor or to a senior member of staff. But it is clear that in your special position as a teaching assistant you may be the first to hear of a problem. You have a duty to inform those senior to you. It can be very difficult for everyone if the first anyone knows about a problem is when the parents come steaming through the door and tell whoever is listening that their son told you about this and still nothing has been done. Always report it. You cannot take responsibility for solving all issues single-handedly. In fact few of us ever attempt to do so. Schools succeed as a result of the teams that are created, not through mavericks.

The feelings we have for our children are part of the common human experience that we all share. It is not something that is only the domain of clean, happy middle-class families.

You must never believe even for a moment that the parents of the most unpleasant child in the school do not share those overwhelming feelings that you have for your own children. Demonize the villain of Year 9 as much as you like, but someone loves him – though in some sad and sorry cases, the tense is wrong. Someone loved him once. The reason why he is naughty now is that no one loves him any longer. You will learn the longer that you spend in school that there is nearly always something to be uncovered about the burdens that our most troubled students carry with them.

We always need to remind ourselves of this when our day gets stressful and tense. We all do it. We stand around and express our dislike for a child and what he has done. We cannot understand how the mother can defend such villainy. But they can. They love their child. They believe their child. Do not ever condemn them for doing so. However blindingly obvious the crimes of their children are, they love their child and want to help them. They are behaving no differently than the rest of us.

7

Governors

Governors are a strange breed. They assume enormous responsibility for the school and receive nothing in return for all the anxiety and the sleepless nights that they will experience. There are occasions when it can be a very stressful experience indeed.

They take the ultimate responsibility for all things in the school – appointing a headteacher in a spirit of great excitement or dismissing a headteacher with Alzheimer's in an atmosphere of tension and anxiety, monitoring the complicated budget that a school must operate, permanently excluding disruptive students. And they do this out of a sense of philanthropy. They are a symbol of the way in which a community takes ownership of its schools. They represent a genuine connection between the school and the community where the children live. You can become a governor yourself. Schools are always looking for interested and supportive people to work with them. Indeed many people in education want to make a further investment in the system by becoming a governor in a local school. It will give you without doubt an entirely different perspective. If you really want to find out how the school machine works then think seriously about it. You will find out how appointments are made, how the curriculum is organized, how the budget is managed. The headteacher will need to write a regular report outlining the work of the school. This is an opportunity to celebrate an achievement or a success. This mixture of scrutiny and celebration is a perfect example of what they do. It is a challenging role and certainly never a dull one. So offer your services. You will have plenty to offer and you will gain a great insight. Instead of being interviewed you could be making the appointment. It can be quite a responsibility.

A governing body should reflect the rich variety of the community that the school serves. There will be local councillors perhaps, representatives from the education authority, parents, teachers and increasingly student representatives.

There will be many subcommittees that deal with specific issues, such as appointments or finance or exclusion or staff discipline. Every part of the school's life is referred to them. Governors who find themselves attached to a particular subject may take a particular interest in how it operates. It is possible that they might be invited to a department meeting to which they can bring their enthusiasm and to which they can offer their scrutiny. They will have an involvement in all policies that frame and underpin the work of the school. The adoption of policies is entirely their duty. They will have legal responsibilities for issues like gender and race equality, bullying and accessibility. They will receive reports on a regular basis. Subcommittees will monitor all aspects of the school's work. They will give their permission for the things that happen in the school, like overseas visits or adventure holidays. And remember always that this ultimate responsibility is entirely unpaid work.

You might find yourself interviewed by an appointments committee drawn from the governing body. They might well defer to the professional expertise of the teachers involved but they may themselves ask questions and of course they bring to their duties their own interests and experiences. In my experience they will ultimately defer to the opinions and preferences of the professionals, but only after quizzing them closely and subjecting their opinions to rigorous scrutiny.

They will often have strong opinions and indeed you might find a parent governor who has a particular interest in special needs issues. They might have a personal investment in the success of this area, through their own child for example. This means that they might have particularly informed knowledge about a specialist area, like dyspraxia for example. You might see the governors around the school quite frequently because ultimately they are like managers and they need to know what is going on in all the different areas.

You do get the occasional local megalomaniac who joins the governing body in order to feed their ego. Their intention generally is to get into the school to 'sort them out'. Of course, they don't. The other governors will hold them in check and dilute their agenda.

We are all answerable to them in our own way. Yet teachers often wonder what the fuss is about. Another governors' meeting? Who cares? But the head cares because they are part of his job. They will have an impact on you because they have an impact upon the school and you will be part of it.

Their scrutiny may require an examination of the effective nature of your deployment and your work. It is not up to them to pass judgement on your professional competence. They might not be qualified to do so, but they can ask questions about where you are being used. You work with children about whom others have concerns and this might bring you to the attention of different stake holders. You will always need to be aware of this. It might be that you will be asked to provide information and insight on the child you support. Who else is able to do so with such informed understanding?

These responsibilities will be moderated. They will fall largely upon the more senior teaching staff but you might need to contribute. After all, your perspective will give you entirely different impressions which could well be the most important ones of all.

Governors also act as ears in the community. They will pick up the word on the street and that word might one day be about you. Any adult who works in school will get talked about by the students and other people will get to hear it. There is rarely ever any anonymity in a secondary school.

Never underestimate the governors. They are good people fulfilling a very demanding role. The more that we demand of schools the greater the demands we make on governors. Sometimes this doesn't seem fair. They are part of the fabric of the school and no member of the school should ever take them for granted.

8

Dealing with behaviour

If after a period of time you start to agree with more reactionary editorials in the press then it is time to get out and do something else. It is very easy for people to demonize young people – although often what they really mean is other people's children. Groups loitering on the street are a threat you won't walk past. They have evil intent. They are sullen, aggressive, drugged, unpredictable. Apart, of course, from my own grandchildren. Of course there are difficult children. They are everywhere. But they are not the majority. They are our children. We have created them. We have given them the world they inhabit – with all its imperfections, it is what our generation has made. They didn't invent mobile phones; they just learned to use them better than us. We have poisoned them through the food we give them; we have created a world of rapidly moving, flickering images; we have promoted drinking and smoking. We have taken their money to profit big business.

And we have said it's their fault.

Of course it's an exaggeration. But pause before you rant about our young people. They live and move in a world that is very different from the one we had – and they have had to adapt as best they can. But they started out just like us.

When you've been in school for a while, think about your own childhood. Is the school that much different? Do you not recognize the behaviour and the attitudes that you see? Possibly you do. People don't really change much across the years; we have more wires and cables today, that's all.

So don't be surprised when nice children smile at you and wish you good morning. Don't be shocked when they hold doors open. They will laugh and cry just like you did. So you must make sure that your opinions are not bent and shaped by the prejudices used to sell newspapers. Of course you will be challenged by what you see. There will be conflict, disagreements, confrontations. Isn't that inevitable when you put all these different people together in one building? They interact with each other everyday in a random fashion. It certainly makes for completely unpredictable relationships. It is chaos theory in action. A sneeze in a French lesson leads to an argument in maths three hours later which means two days later that the Year 7 girls football team are beaten on penalties and as a result Natalie swears at you on Friday morning. It happens.

What you need to do is to preserve a sense of proportion and largely remain calm as much as you can. Righteous anger has its place and can be very effective – as long as you don't use it too often.

If you do that you become a figure of fun and children will seek you out to see you perform. In the end that's the trick: staying calm. I don't mean that you should be a doormat. But don't let yourself look foolish. Maintain dignity. Poor behaviour disappoints you, it doesn't drive you into a frenzy.

One of the most important things you need to do is to acquaint yourself with the school's behaviour policy. This should contain, in clear language, four important features:

- Rights
- Responsibilities
- Rules
- Routines

There will also be a sense of consequences. But all schools and the adults working in them must promote the basic right to learn in a safe and supported environment where they will be treated with respect. In this atmosphere you hope they will develop their skills to become useful, productive and happy adults.

This sense of consequences impacts upon you too. You can ask a student to come back to see you at lunchtime. It could be for either positive or negative reasons. But you have to be sure that you are there to meet them. Because if you are not, then your credibility will start to erode.

So what sorts of challenging behaviour might you encounter? Well, the vast majority will be low-level and irritating disruption. Talking out of turn, walking around the classroom, failing to concentrate upon the purposes of the lesson. Low-level yes. But high-frequency. And the cumulative effect will be to disrupt the learning process.

There will be further disruption when the behaviour leads to arguments, accusations, denials. What we really need to do is to concentrate upon the cause and deal with that before it develops into anything else.

The trick is to plan always for good behaviour. You need to give out the message that anything else puzzles you.

Always make sure that the students you deal with are always aware of the consequences of the things that they do. This is something that many young people find difficult to grasp. They struggle to recognize how one action leads inevitably to another. In some way they see events as being self-contained and separate, when to you anyway they are clearly interconnected. So they have to see that if they do something it will provoke a consequence. It is part of growing up.

An important stage along the way is praise. It is a sad fact that many students rarely hear a word of approval or encouragement either at school or at home. One of the most important tasks you will perform is to praise the students. You must show them that you appreciate their efforts and their struggles. By promoting positive behaviour you are helping them to develop a sense of consequences. Meaningful praise in a realistic context is vital in developing relationships and in managing behaviour.

You must always be realistic in what you say, but there are always opportunities to promote achievement.

This is a difficult piece of work we have been asked to do now but I am really confident that you will do well. You did some very good work yesterday and I know that you can do it again, especially because I'm here to help you.

If you want to effect a change in anyone's behaviour then forcing them by your actions is always an external pressure. Persuading and directing through well-chosen words is an internal pressure and always more effective because it is more long-lasting.

Naturally things won't always go perfectly. But always remember that there are alternatives to confrontation. Humour can often defuse a difficult situation, as long as it is well judged. Insults and sarcasm can only work if a relationship has been previously established. It is often very effective to keep on repeating instructions in a calm voice until you get a response, like a dodgy CD. It can also be effective to discreetly move away from a student in the classroom who is angry, on the pretext of helping someone else. In this way you will not be seen to be backing down and you will give the student time and space to calm themselves. There is nothing clever here, just basic human interaction. And of course the most important thing of all is to be ready to seek support from other adults around you. This is not weakness; it is something that all those working in school must do at sometime. None of us should ever be too proud to do so.

It is also important that we listen carefully to our students, that we give them a right of reply and that we are always ready to apologize when we get things wrong.

When you have had a disagreement, then you, as an adult, have to be ready to move on. You need to forgive, to put issues behind you, to focus on positive things. So look for something the student has done well as soon as possible after the disagreement. In this way you will be shifting the emphasis from the negative straight onto the positive. You can't let students feel that because they get something wrong once, they will never again get anything right. So it is up to you, however personally aggrieved you feel, to restore and renew the relationship.

In a secondary school you might be the one consistent adult in an ever-changing world. You might be the only adult with whom they have a consistent relationship. This is a really important part of your job. It gives you an overall perspective on the child in the school across a range of subjects. This means that you can compare behaviour in one situation with that in another. You can remind them of their obligations, their previous successes. You can be a kind of eye in the sky. You can see common issues that might provoke particular difficulties or indeed predict when a problem might be about to happen.

This ability to compare is really important – because it joins up the experiences in school and develops a sense of consequence. Why be naughty in history when earlier in the day you were good in French?

Children need to feel valued as individuals and encouraged to achieve. A teaching assistant has a huge part to play in all this.

Something that plays a really important part here is language. The choice of words that we use can influence how others react and behave. You will remember good teachers, not always because of what they said but often because of the way they said it. You can encourage students and defuse situations through the words that you use. So you need to focus on what the student does well and draw examples from it. It works for adults. Why not for students?

So don't criticize them for not doing their maths homework. 'You forgot your homework again!' No, it is usually far more productive to say, 'You did really well to finish your science homework last week. Now you need to do the same in maths'. This is another example of how your perspective can help by drawing the whole-school experience together. It is always useful to reflect upon your own experience, both good and bad. The very best teachers had something to say and did it in a way that was easy to understand. They had the gift of making what they said sound interesting. They seemed to enjoy the presence of their students in the classroom. The students were pleased to be with them and talked about their lessons and what they did. It is all about tone and language and respect.

Such people have a gift and we can't all hope to find it in ourselves. But we can model ourselves upon some of the things that they do. One thing that you will notice in the very best teachers is that they expect good behaviour. They are not confrontational at all. In fact they appear genuinely shocked if their students are not engaged and cooperative. They do not appear to anticipate a problem – because they have planned carefully. You can learn from this. If you know something causes a student to behave badly – like a packet of crisps at break time or a fizzy drink – then do something to prevent it. Don't react to circumstances; control them by planning. In this way everyone benefits from a lack of disruption. It maintains focus for everyone. And it is true that praise works. Make your students feel good about themselves and they will feel good about you. They will want to work with you and as a result they will show the sort of improvements that will make you feel you are doing a proper and a successful job.

9

What do you think you should do?

You cannot predict what will happen to you in school. That is the beauty of working in one. No two days are ever the same. Just when you thought you'd got the job sorted in your own mind, something else turns up that can turn your day – and you – completely upside down. It is inevitable because people do unpredictable things and a school is full of small, complicated and unpredictable children. There will be many occasions when you have nothing to model your reactions on because you will be dealing with something you haven't come across before. You will therefore need to use your instincts and your experience to find your way through the unfamiliar, while at the same time following established school procedures.

So what I have done here is to outline ten different issues, all of which are real, all of which I have had to deal with myself in school. It is the stuff of my working life and the lives of everyone who spends time in a secondary school. None of them is a drama. They are just my job.

You might find it useful to examine each one of these in turn and think about what you might have done in such a situation. Then, look at what I did or what I think you should do. I am not saying that I am always right, because I got some of them wrong the first time. But if it happened in my school then it might happen to you. It will also give you some idea of the sort of thing that can happen in secondary schools if you haven't been in one for a while.

Think carefully about these situations. They are real and they are quite likely to arise in some form or other during your career. If you think I am making this sort of thing up, then get real. You are not ready for even a day in a normal school.

When such issues do happen you are likely to react instinctively, though informed by a sense of what is proper and appropriate. But it is good to think about such issues in advance and compare your responses with those of others around you.

But there is always, of course, more than one answer to these dilemmas. It is hard to divorce them completely from the context in which they happened and your answers will be generally hypothetical, since the individuals can never be properly known to you. But the basic answer to any of them is that before you do anything you should stop and think. You are an adult dealing with children and sometimes the right way to deal with things requires nothing more than a moment's reflection, followed by a liberal application of common sense. The other thing of course is never to try to deal with an issue on your own. Refer it on to someone else, talk to a colleague. In your desire to help, you can get yourself in far too deep, far too quickly.

So look at these incidents here and form an impression of my working day. One day this world could be yours.

1. Two girls you don't know are fighting in the corridor. What do you do?
2. A boy you are assisting tells you there was a boy in the toilet who offered him drugs. What do you do?
3. A girl you don't know tells you to 'f' off. How do you respond?
4. An angry and verbally abusive parent appears in the corridor.
5. A child tells you that a teacher has pushed him around.

6. You watch a teacher repeatedly having difficulty in the classroom.
7. A child wants to have your mobile phone number so that they can talk to you because things are difficult at home.
8. The girl you support is rarely in school. You believe she is being kept at home to look after a child.
9. You think the boy you support has been shoplifting.
10. A teacher repeatedly asks you to look after a class while they disappear, apparently to the staffroom.

In all these circumstances the first thing you must do is to realize that you can't solve any of these issues on your own. You are going to need the support of senior and more experienced colleagues. But the first question is a good example of an occasion when you have to take responsibility. You can't walk away. Get between the girls and try to grab hold of their arms to prevent them causing any damage to each other. The problem you might have is that it is a lot harder to stop girls from fighting than boys. Boys will generally step back and friends will intervene to prevent any further blows. Girls are usually more vicious. Ask the other children around for help and send one to get a senior colleague who is close by. It helps if you know the name of a child in the crowd. (There are always spectators.) Don't let go of the girls and try to lead them away from the scene if possible. But all you can do is to hold on and wait for the cavalry to arrive.

Clearly in question two you need to refer this on as soon as possible. You don't know if they really were drugs but of course you don't know they are not. So speak immediately to the classroom teacher and together call upon the pastoral team leader. Support the boy and stay with him when he is being interviewed by senior staff especially if he is required to write anything down. It might be that he knows the name of the boy but is frightened and is only prepared to pass on the name to someone he trusts and that person might well be you.

There are a number of possible responses to question three and the shocked response that leads immediately to ranting and raving is the least productive. You will look foolish. Shouting out angrily 'What did you say?' might actually provoke a repetition! It is after all what you have just asked for. But ignoring it is not an option. If you do, you have given the girl a licence to say what she wants and given her pals the encouragement they need to have a go next. So you are shocked and disappointed and you want to discuss the matter immediately and in private. Don't do it in the corridor when there is an audience enjoying your discomfort and behaving as excited teenage groups can behave. No, the best place is in your space and on your terms. But also tell a teacher or a pastoral worker. You don't know if this is a one-off incident or whether it is happening regularly. Perhaps the girl doesn't know what she is saying. You don't know. You only see part of the picture. Someone else sees a great deal more.

Never confront anyone alone if you find yourself in the situation that number four describes. You have no way of knowing the condition or the mental health of the person who is in front of you. Always be unfailingly polite and offer to escort the parent to the school office where they can properly be received into the school. If it is possible send for help – a good way actually is to stop a child and ask them to take a completely random object to a teacher close by. It disguises the fact that you have sent for help. Staff should have been briefed to respond in such circumstances. It is a hard one to deal with because you should never put yourself at risk but at the same time you need to protect the children around you. But you need to get them out of the corridors and into an office somewhere with a senior member of staff. It is their problem.

Number five is an interesting situation because you have to take the child's word in the first instance and accept that they want to make a complaint. You tell the child that you have to tell someone and that they will probably ask them questions. Since this is a formal complaint you might need to help them frame their thoughts, especially if the child has learning difficulties. There is a whole machinery that cranks into action in these circumstances and you have few choices to make. You cannot keep it to yourself: you are obliged to inform someone else and these procedures should have been outlined to you during your induction. It is up to the headteacher to make the judgement about whether there is any substance to these allegations, not you.

There are many reasons why a teacher may be having difficulties as indicated in number six. There could be a significant mismatch between the abilities of the teacher and the nature of the class that has been developing for some time. It could be that the teacher is going through some sort of health difficulty or domestic problem. Members of the class might have decided to target him or her deliberately and maliciously. Whatever the reason, your job should be to tell your immediate superior that you are aware of this. Don't go to the teacher's superior since your observations might not be welcomed since you could be regarded as an outsider. You could obviously talk gently to the teacher about how difficult the class has become and give them the opportunity to open up but real solutions to the issue lie outside your area of expertise. Let the professionals deal with it.

Number seven? Obviously you never give any personal contact details to a child in any circumstances. Mobile phone number, email address, nothing. To do so is to strap yourself to the front of the Disaster Express. Of course the child can talk to you, but only in the structured environment of school and you can never guarantee that you will not pass on what you are told. You cannot take that sort of responsibility. You tell them that you will listen, of course you will. But you can never make any promises. It is your professional responsibility to make sure that if there really is a genuine problem that the appropriate responses are put in place. So tell the person with responsibility for child protection straightaway. It is vitally important that you know who this is and it has to be an essential part of the induction programme.

In any similar circumstance to that outlined in number eight you need to inform someone of your concerns straightaway. That would need to be a member of the pastoral support team and probably the educational welfare officer for the school. These sorts of things often happen, either because of parental incompetence or parental desperation. It is often a shock to have to confront the reality of the conditions under which many of the children in our poorest areas have to live. Their future is often compromised because the parent can see no other alternative. It is not always condemnation that they need but rather support.

As far as the shoplifter is concerned there are a range of issues that this can raise. Obviously you need to share your concerns at the earliest opportunity so that proper investigations can be carried out. Why is it happening? Is the boy being coerced into doing it by others? Is he being bullied? Is he stealing sweets to sell them? If so, why does he need the money? Lots of issues can suddenly emerge if the situation is handled carefully. Once again, that is why you need to leave it in the hands of those with greater experience. However, do not forget that your relationship with the child could be a decisive and influential factor. They might always need you there.

Number ten is an easy one to deal with. It is wrong and it shouldn't happen. It is not why you have been employed, to provide whole-class cover. Obviously there can be occasional issues that arise which might mean that you are left alone in the room. For example, if the teacher you are working with is a head of department then they may well be called away from time to time. But if it happens frequently and you feel that someone is taking advantage, then tell your line manager. It needs to be dealt with. It is not fair on you, no matter how competent you are, and it is certainly not fair on the students.

Your objective in any such dilemma ultimately must be to solve a problem for the benefit of the child and, sometimes in order to do so, you need to enlist the help and status of someone else. But if you are the first on the scene or a disclosure is made to you, you need to respond immediately.

Your position as a teaching assistant in the school is an important one. Never underestimate the influence you can have. You will form close relationships with students. They will feel confident and comfortable in your presence. As a result of this, they will tell you things. You will find things out. And you will learn to listen to the children very carefully and never to dismiss what they say to you straightaway.

There will be many other issues that you will need to address in school as your career there unfolds but these examples here should give you some sort of idea of a framework within which you can determine your responses. It is always interesting, and entertaining, to ask other teaching assistant colleagues what their biggest problems have been and how they dealt with them. Listen carefully to what they have to say. Did they get it right? Or did they get it wrong? What were the consequences? Think about what you would have done in similar circumstances. This can be a very good training exercise and a good way of carrying out inductions for new members of staff – just as long as you don't manage to put them off completely!

10

Working with the learning advice department

The inclusion agenda is an important thread to your induction because this is where your job originated. And the inclusion agenda, which has a chapter all of its own, is at the heart of the learning advice department.

All children have equal worth, but they don't all have similar experiences and sadly many are disadvantaged by what has happened to them. Part of your role is to redress that balance as much as you can. Of course, we all have a moral obligation to do so but there is also a more practical reason why it is important. Disadvantage and exclusion for children has an enormous social consequence in later years. If problems are not addressed then there are huge implications for underachievement and social dysfunction. Where do the majority of criminals come from? The prison population depends particularly upon those from troubled childhoods. Exclude children from school for their behaviour for example and often, quite simply, you destroy their life. We can thus condemn them to an unstructured and vulnerable life on the streets, with all that this implies.

Of course if you don't exclude them, then you might in return destroy someone else. So there are no quick fixes here. We have to work with all the children in our schools and give all of them the opportunities that will help them grow and create sustainable communities.

You can be part of the team that does this. It is an indication of the wider role that school plays in our society and the many purposes that it is perceived to fulfil. When it starts to deal with these issues, then it places your job at the very heart of the process. Because whatever happens in our world also happens in the classroom. Schools merely model what it is that takes place elsewhere. This makes them vibrant and exciting places. But it can also make them edgy and dangerous. The learning advice department is certainly on the front line.

You might spend some considerable time working with students who are learning English as an additional language. You might well need more information about ethnic minority achievement. This is a fascinating area, and a very rewarding one, giving you an unexpected and invaluable insight into other cultures. It is the sort of experience that is very likely to change your own outlook completely. You are likely to find an overwhelming commitment to work and a tremendous thirst for improvement. They will demand your expertise and your time and you will be happy to give it.

As we shall see in the next chapter, inclusion isn't just about stopping students being excluded. It is about a school creating a secure and collaborative community where everyone is respected and valued. In this way it will promote achievement and social cohesion.

Your base might always be in the learning advice department and it is where you may need to report as your day evolves. There will be occasions when a child to whom you are attached will be away from school and therefore you will need to be reassigned. It could be that you will support a teacher for the day or support a different child who may have needs which are perhaps slightly marginal and don't require regular attention. You might be able to spend a day preparing materials or working with a small group of learners withdrawn from lessons for this purpose. Your line manager will make this decision but don't be afraid to offer an opinion on the basis of what you have seen. It may be that you will be aware of something that should be addressed that you have seen as you have observed lessons and classes. Never forget that you have a different perspective on what happens in the school.

But schools are such places that you must always offer yourself for work if you are unexpectedly free. They are busy and pressurized and operate at their best on the basis of mutual support and teamwork. To make an easy day for yourself is generally to make someone else's day harder. So never hide away. Offer yourself, and in that way you will earn the proper respect of the others around you.

It is always helpful I think to involve yourself as much as possible with the wider work of the department. It may be that this will give you an opportunity to work with a wider range of students. You should do this to enhance your understanding and it could prove to be particularly informative if you are anticipating moving into a teaching career at some point. You may have a chance to meet the most gifted in the school and those who are most disadvantaged. Your job description may have allocated you to a particular student and that may be an ongoing commitment for a number of years, but it may not last forever and you do need to form an impression of the extent of the department's work.

You will find some very good and thoughtful teachers in learning advice departments. They will be either dedicated specialists or sometimes teachers from other subject areas who have been re-deployed into the subject. They will bring with them the knowledge and framework that their original subject gave them. This can make the department very rich and wide-ranging. The old days where superannuated teachers, past their sell-by date, were put out to grass in the department have long since gone. Now they are staffed largely by committed teachers with relevant training and expertise in specialist areas like dyslexia and behaviour management. You can learn a lot from these people, particularly since they may be experienced staff who have a good track record in dealing with behaviour issues, something that can exercise teaching assistants everywhere.

Of course, the department is not only a base for adults in the school. It needs to become a base for the students too. It can be very successful if the department sets up a base that the children who receive their support can use at lunchtime. It could be a welcome refuge from the bustle of the day and give students a chance to reflect and socialize, because of course they may need to develop their social skills, which can often be a little limited. This would provide them with a secure environment in which to do so. It could also be very rewarding and productive for teaching assistants and the students they support to meet at lunchtime so that they can talk about many different issues. They might be able to talk about the work they have had to do and any difficulties it has presented. Solutions would then be easy to discuss away from the pressure of the classroom. Future worries can be explored, concerns aired. This is probably the only context in which these discussions can take place. If a lunchtime club of this sort does not already exist then perhaps this could be your own personal contribution to the department. All you would need is a comfortable area into which you could introduce interesting resources like books and magazines, a few posters, perhaps some bottled water, perhaps some music too, although you should choose it to create the right ambience. You don't want thumping disco beats when you are trying to be thoughtful! The other thing that this does is make the children within the department feel special and stops them from becoming isolated. They can see that they are part of a larger group, that there is a continuum and they can see the successes of others. Make it a special base and the daily lives of the students will be enhanced.

11

Inclusion

Inclusion is a very wide-ranging concept. It embraces all aspects of the life of the school because the principle it outlines is that all children should have equal access to all the opportunities that a proper education can provide. It is a simple idea but once accepted then it touches every part of what we do. So the concept of inclusion is not only about preventing its opposite, which is exclusion. It is about creating a stimulating and enhancing school community in which everyone feels they have a part to play. Everyone is part of the whole-school community and they can contribute, no matter what their attainment, gender or race. No one is a less important part of the whole; the school belongs to all its members and we need to recognize that.

The curriculum should therefore treat all students in a similar way, providing challenges, surprises and enjoyment. Through the experiences they are offered, the students should be invited to remove barriers, not erect them. This means that all those in the school should contribute to the creation of a proper climate and tone, based upon mutual regard and respect. There should be no place for fear, intimidation and aggression.

Of course, all students are different. They must never be regarded as having no individuality or no right to contribute. They all need opportunities to progress, and for some this might involve speech and language therapy or physiotherapy, but they must be given the same opportunities as everyone else in the school. They should not, for example, be excluded from an important school trip merely upon the basis of their learning needs. Reasonable adaptations and adjustments should be made to ensure full involvement in every aspect of school.

As a teaching assistant you might be assigned to a student with particular needs and, as a result of this, you will learn a huge amount about this condition. You may need to consider whether you would like to become an expert in this specialist field and certainly you would have every opportunity to become so. And while it might seem wrong to regard such a misfortune as a career opportunity, nonetheless it could bring enormous benefits to very many other students. You could become the teaching assistant in the school with expertise in dyslexia for example. As a result you will be able to offer informed help to many others.

The work you do as a teaching assistant should increase the extent to which all students can take advantage of educational opportunities. You have a really significant part to play in this. You need to be a champion for all those who are disadvantaged in any way, thus ensuring that no discrimination takes place either in the classroom or in the wider school. You will want your student to be fully involved in all aspects of the school and in this belief you will be connecting to a wider and universal set of values. The United Nations Convention on the Rights of the Child in 1989 said:

Every child has the right to live free from discrimination.

What right has your school to stand outside such a declaration?

Of course, schools can be harsh places and children sometimes rather assertive and lacking in sensitivity. As a result you need to promote a sense of inclusion on behalf of your students. Schools are not only about confirming attitudes; they should also be involved in changing unnecessary ones. So it is crucial in schools that children are taught the importance of valuing differences, whether they are physical, intellectual or spiritual. A culture that excludes such things is doomed to failure. We must always diversify and invite everyone to make a contribution.

An included person feels valued, happy and useful. An excluded person feels rejected, angry and unhappy. Why should we ever wish such feelings upon anyone? And of course to include someone is certainly the choice to make if you want to improve and encourage their learning.

Naturally, you must ensure that you clear your own mind of any prejudices you might have. You must always have a clear and open mind and give that message to those around you. Remember you are a role model and a child will always hear and repeat a comment made in an unguarded moment. You can guarantee it. So watch what you say. Keep any extreme opinions to yourself.

So a school must have high expectations of everyone. It must celebrate diversity; it must always be positive. The role you have is crucial in this.

Clearly in a specialist world where you are acquiring and developing the skills you need to deal with defined issues, you will need focused training. If you find yourself working with those with a visual or a hearing impairment you will need to find particular courses. It is the same if you are assigned to asylum seeker children. You will need to acquire skills in providing English for use in different contexts, both in social situations and in the classroom.

Remember, you will always need training. You are not the finished article. Not one of us ever is. So you will need to maintain your skills. The most important part of this is that you show the willingness to adapt and to learn new things. And to find or adapt new resources.

You will need to explore the current position about statements of special educational needs (SENs). The importance of school action programmes and a detailed analysis falls outside the scope of this book. However, essentially, statements are legal documents outlining provision and are reserved for those with the most severe and complex needs that are likely to persist beyond school. The majority of those with special educational needs are supported without statements in school. This is school action. There are also those students who receive school action plus, where specialist provision like a speech therapist or a behaviour specialist, is provided.

The actions that a school has taken that are different from those in place for the rest of the class are recorded in an Individual Education Plan (IEP). These are tools that aid preparation. There is every possibility that a teaching assistant might be involved in drawing up such a plan and certainly they would be involved in its implementation.

In all situations you will find that particular resources can help students to access parts of their education. This is obviously true of computer-based learning programmes that can do so much to expand the work of the classroom. They can provide individual and focused solutions to learning issues and in a way they are just like a good teaching assistant, in that they remove barriers to learning. So you need to keep aware of developments in this area at all times. Computers will never replace you, but they can certainly enhance what you do.

There are always things that computers cannot do because they do not deal with the intricacies of people in the way that you can. Difficulties in forming relationships, in organizing themselves, in expressing themselves, will always impact upon the success of the learning process. These difficulties may occur in one particular area or be severe and permanent difficulties. In your role, working closely with students, you can begin to find ways of reducing the impact of problems and promoting success. You were appointed to remove barriers to learning and that should always be at the front of your mind. Some children find it harder to learn some things than others. So they will need extra help. It is estimated that about 17 per cent of all students will have a special educational need at some time or other. There are different ways of responding to this. Appointing more support staff may not, in fact, be the complete answer. Sometimes what they will need is material that is designed exclusively for them or indeed special equipment. It might not necessarily be your job to find the equipment, but you can make a real impact in adapting materials. You will need to work together with teachers to create effective learning situations and you will do this by making sure that all students are involved in the business of the classroom.

There are many adaptations you can make that will have an impact.

You can adapt the number of things that a learner has to learn. You can give them more time to complete things, you can intervene to a greater or lesser extent, by writing a sentence or two to make the task less daunting. What you need to do is to be very sensitive to the needs of the student. You can provide key words, you can provide prompts, but your role isn't to do the work. Your role is to improve the context so that the student can complete it successfully.

You might be there in practical lessons to reinforce health and safety issues. This is a very important role that is much valued by teachers, since in workshops and laboratories a teaching assistant can act as an extra 'pair of eyes' in situations that can be challenging or dangerous.

A teaching assistant could find themselves as part of a multi-agency team dealing with the needs of a child and their family. It is quite a shock to suddenly find yourself drawn into issues at such a specialist level. It should emphasize the real importance of the job that you do. No one will work quite so closely with a child as you will and no one else will form the insights that you have. You might of course be involved in some of the therapies that are recommended for children. You might be encouraging a child to carry out certain physiotherapy exercises; you might be involved in intensive work to improve speech production. Your feedback on the effectiveness of these therapies will be very important. You might have to submit either oral or written reports and you should be ready for this. You might also need to explain things to parents who will look upon you as someone with specialist knowledge and skills who is, most importantly of all, on their side.

There will always be those students who have considerable needs if they are to progress. These needs may have a specific nature. It is important therefore that you come to terms with the implications of disabilities. Some children with disabilities will have no difficulties in learning and may require no help at all. They will not have any SEN; they will only be disabled. Of course, their rights need to be protected and they should not be treated any less favourably than anyone else without justification. You will need to have some understanding of the various conditions that are present within the student body and how they should be managed. The key, quite naturally, is that information is available and shared.

You will undoubtedly come across students with ADHD, a condition of children who have long-term difficulties with attention, hyperactivity and impulsive behaviour. They can find it difficult to plan and control their reactions to things. They find it hard to concentrate and pay attention. It can be a very frustrating condition and is often controlled by medication designed to help then focus.

You can provide a framework for them, by repeating instructions, rewarding good behaviour and giving sanctions when it is poor, by remaining calm and consistent. This is a common condition in secondary schools and one you should keep yourself informed about. Asperger syndrome, autism spectrum disorders, cerebral palsy, Down syndrome, dyslexia, dyspraxia, hearing impairment and visual impairment are all specific conditions that you may encounter. The learning advice department should have access to the detailed information that you might require to enable you to provide the appropriate sort of support. Never forget, that in terms of making reasonable adjustments to enable a student with disabilities to access the school curriculum, then your appointment should have been a key moment. Yours is a job that comes with responsibility. It is up to you to ensure that the school maintains an inclusive approach and resolves learning issues as professionally as possible for all students, whatever sort of problems they present. There are nearly 300,000 students in secondary schools in 2007 for whom English is an additional language. It is something that you will certainly come across. Some teaching assistants are employed specifically to support students from minority ethnic groups but whether you are one of these or not, all can support the acquisition of language.

To become fluent in another language can take a long time. It can take on average five to seven years to become fully competent. And we don't just expect students to acquire the language – we expect them to develop academic language needed for success in examinations and coursework. You will have a role to play here. You should familiarize yourself with the numbers involved in your school, what sort of languages are spoken at home, are these expected to change, are there any experienced speakers of these languages in the community who can be called upon to help with difficulties that might arise?

Valuable opportunities for language learning occur not only in lessons but at all times of the day in many different interactions. Our schools have an increasing diversity of languages within them and an awareness of how the development of English skills can be promoted will be very useful. Of course, language can be developed in all subjects. That used in maths and science can be very rich and very valuable, especially since some of the concepts within those subjects themselves are not language specific. One plus four is always five, and this truth could be used as the basis for language acquisition.

A central feature however is interaction with others, both students and adults. Full involvement in the richness of the curriculum will provide plenty of opportunities for language to develop, especially with the support and intervention of a teaching assistant. At home, like all of us, they learned their first language happily, in a stress-free environment by interacting with adults who cared for them. It is the natural way of doing it. It we cannot replicate part of that in schools, then language acquisition will always be more haphazard. They will look to you for the security they need. You will need to act as a mediator, to involve them in oral discussions, to provide models of consistent English language use.

Of course, learners benefit from taking part in whole-class and group activities where you can offer focused support. You can repeat the teacher's message, explain things, encourage involvement through correct responses.

There are many things you can do to help. You will need to be involved in the lesson preparation for example so that you can identify and highlight key words. You should always make sure that your student can see the whiteboard and the teacher clearly. Always make sure you have a dictionary available. You can also take an interest in their first language and culture. It is something to be celebrated and promoted. This will have a great influence on their self-esteem and their sense of the important part they can play in the school community as a whole. If possible you can find and use traditional stories from their community, because what they have and what they know must be given proper status. Clearly this is a specialist area and your colleagues should have access to the sort of material and training that will be useful to you. But the most important thing that you can have is a positive attitude to the concept of bilingualism.

You will get to know a student and be able to familiarize them with the routines of school life. You will be a constant presence in an ever-changing and bewildering, alien world. Many students throughout our secondary schools have low self-esteem and so it is really important that you work to develop positive relationships that they can use to increase their confidence. A teaching assistant can provide an important listening space and boost status by being an adult who is interested in them. You could indeed become a genuine life-enhancing experience.

12

Teaching assistants and the digital age

You cannot escape from it. It is everywhere and it dominates the lives of us all. And it is ever-changing, never still. You have to master it or at least establish a relationship with it or you will never be able to do your job properly. Or indeed any job properly. There may have been a time when it was not essential but that time has long gone. I am taking of course about the computer and other aspects of the digital world in which we live.

School management and teaching are based entirely upon them. Record keeping and assessment procedures are all computer based. The tracking of behaviour and incidents, attendance and reporting are all carried out electronically. Individual Educational Plans are stored and accessed. You will find that in many schools, parents are sent a text message immediately their child is absent or missing. They no longer have to wait for a letter arriving three days later. Everything is becoming instant and traceable. You will become part of the system and one of the very good things about working in a school is that it does keep you up to date to some extent with new technology. I am sure I am only conversant with the basic operations of mobile phones and MP3 players because I work with young people. And of course they all know much more than me – and that is in some ways a problem. They can hide things from me and baffle me with their expertise. I am not the only one who experiences these things and really there is not much we can do about it. It is essential for the relationship between the generations that there are some parts of it that cannot be penetrated by oldies like ourselves. Communications, music sharing, video – all those things will go far beyond our grasp. We shouldn't worry about it. We are supposed to fail in these areas. We need to make sure that we can use ICT, not for leisure, but as a learning tool and a support to organization. Clearly word processing is a vital skill you must acquire, along with research methods, spreadsheets and databases. Manipulating images is also a useful skill when preparing attractive worksheets.

There are many other ways in which the computer can actually help you in your job. You can access advice and training both within the school from the intranet and outside the school from the internet. You need to know about these opportunities and share any discoveries with your colleagues. Work can be prepared and made available for other teaching assistants and so developed and improved through experience.

This is an interesting point, since an important part of your work will be to develop resources that can help students deal with difficult and new concepts and it is always a shame if such work hasn't been saved and shared. The teaching assistants should have their own particular space on the school system where they can store their work. If you can access these things from home as well, then it can be extremely useful for lesson preparation and for reflection. It is one of the things you will soon learn about working in school. The work never goes away from you. You will want to do some work at home out of dedication and out of interest. A properly used computer system can make everything so much easier and effective.

You can design professional quality work very simply, with effective illustrations and cross-referencing that will enhance the learning process. So never turn down any opportunities for training in this area. You will never be completely up to date but neither should you ever fall completely behind.

The other highly significant issue that you will need to address is of course that of child safety in the digital world. It is a huge issue. They adapt to the use of new technologies very quickly. Young people seem to know the way something operates almost instantly without needing to consult the instructions. They represent the biggest market so their needs are the ones which are most often met. And yet this brings with it a problem. They have the dexterity and the instinct to use these things but they don't always have the maturity to understand the implications of what they are doing. They use sophisticated systems in an innocent and inexperienced way. Of course there will always be those children who know things that the adults do not. And they will become adept at hiding what they do. They have completely taken over instant messenger services for example, and social networking appears to many children to be the sole reason why computers were invented.

The internet is a wonderful development, rich with so very many fantastic opportunities. Yet it also has dangers and children will often expose themselves to these dangers thoughtlessly, out of the young person's belief in their own immortality. They will take huge risks, exchanging personal details and photographs with contacts they have never met and who they accept at face value. It is one of the key responsibilities of all adults in the school to teach internet safety and to promote acceptable use policies.

All children can become involved in these things. The world has changed and in ways that many of us are only just beginning to realize. Children now gather together online, rather than on street corners, and this makes them far more vulnerable to predators of many different kinds. Since the majority of children have internet access in their bedrooms (the most recent estimate I have from July 2007 is 80 per cent) they are thus networking in the place where they feel safest and so are always ready to take risks. The computer and the mobile phone are now also two of the biggest arenas for bullying and this has resulted in some surprising consequences. The most unusual one is that it is no longer so easy to identify who the bullies actually are. In the past the physical bully may have been a lot easier to identify. Now, with the use of pseudonyms or false identities, it is not so easy. Cyber bullying adds a whole new dimension. Who is sending those messages either on the phone or on the internet? And the person sending those messages has a perception of their own anonymity which allows them to say things they wouldn't ever say face to face. Not only that, they cannot see the effect of what they are doing, so they lack empathy for others around them. It goes on without stopping and it lasts online forever. You can run away from a physical bully but you cannot escape from the bully who pursues you from the comfort of their own bedroom. And of course that bully may not be the big brute of a boy who wanders around the school yard. It could be that strange little girl who never talks and has no friends.

Since you will often be dealing with the most vulnerable members of the school community you need to be ready to deal with the consequences of any abuse of new technology. You must encourage all students to report what happens to them. They must not keep it quiet. Make sure that they know how to save the evidence in the form of messages and texts. Make sure also that you are familiar with the school's anti-bullying policy, which should have been updated to cover these new threats.

But of course the biggest danger presented by the internet is that we could become far too focused on such threats and forget the massive benefits that it offers us all. Children need to be encouraged to use it sensibly and profitably, not to exploit it for unpleasant reasons. Many children will be allocated a laptop to help them in their studies and as a teaching assistant you might be expected to have some basic understanding of how it operates so that you can provide instant classroom support. Many of the sort of students you will be dealing with will have poor organizational skills and you will need to ensure that they make adequate back-up copies of their work. They might not be able to see ahead far enough to understand the consequences of losing important work. How can things possibly go wrong? Only old people worry. So make sure there's a back-up, and one that can be found so give it a sensible name. It prevents tears before bedtime. Sometimes it is best to be boring.

13

Security

Security and child safety have become almost a national obsession. Each isolated example of a breach or a threat can sometimes be exaggerated by the press into a national disaster. I always feel that we need to keep a perspective. In the overwhelming majority of schools, security issues are never in fact any sort of issue. But every time something happens we are suddenly thrown into 'what if' speculation which isn't terribly helpful. Today primary schools are locked and allegedly secure, although I can usually get in whenever I go on a liaison meeting without too much trouble, and usually on the flimsy basis that I am wearing a suit so I must be official. There may be locks on the door but they will never prevent a person with a grudge getting inside. All they can ever do is slow someone down.

We now live in a world where infant schools are monitored more closely than international frontiers. Children cannot play in the yard at the end of school: they must be passed on individually to a specific and recognized person. They are a commodity that must be exchanged formally, like captured secret agents exchanged among the barbed wire of a misty and forlorn eastern European border.

Yet I worry about the effect this might have upon the minds of the children who are working inside our schools. What messages do they take from our own adult anxieties?

How will it impact upon the way in which they view the world? The world seemed much easier when I was a child, much less constrained. Teaching and learning should be expanding and energizing experiences, not ones carried out as if in a secure establishment, in a sense of fear and anxiety.

Secondary schools can never be as secure or as easily contained as other places. You cannot monitor every entrance and exit. They were designed like sieves to let the students out quickly. Apparently my school has 38 different access points. If you are so minded, you can turn that on its head and say that each of those doors that the children know so well could be an entrance for a nutter with an issue, especially if that nutter is an ex-pupil of the school who knows where to find the person he is looking for. But what we need to do is to keep a perspective on things. How often is it a real possibility? Should we really arrange our schools on the basis of something that is as statistically probable as alien abduction? I don't know, but for many people the threats and dangers are very real and as a professional adult in school, you need to be aware of possible dangers and your responsibilities in challenging circumstances. There are safety implications that attach themselves to many of the different people who use a school and, as a teaching assistant, you need to know what your responsibilities are. This should be outlined to you during your induction process. If you are not clear at the end of it what you need to do then you should seek clarification.

In the first place the issues about child safety must acknowledge the things that the children do themselves. At secondary-school age children are at that stage when they want to take the most risks. They appear to feel that nothing can touch them. They play on railway lines, they throw themselves into rivers. Concerns for their safety are seen as irrelevant. It is in such a way that some start to drink and smoke and take other drugs. The children you deal with might be far more vulnerable than others and may be ready to take more risks in order to impress their friends – or those they would like to be their friends. You will need to reinforce health and security messages at all times. This might require you to speak to your student outside lesson time, perhaps at lunchtime if there are issues that are starting to concern you. Be ready to exploit the specialist help that exists around schools everywhere, in smoking cessation groups and sexual health clinics for example.

Clearly all schools have programmes to deal with safety issues and your role is to support the school in this respect. Messages need to be reinforced at all times and they need to be an integrated part of work and conversations in all aspects of the curriculum.

We all believe that schools should be accessible, at the heart of the communities that they serve. That is how we want them to be. But this brings with it some additional problems. You will often find parents nipping up to school to deal with an apparently trivial issue. And if you live close to the school you will still be steamed up when you get there. You may well be surprised at the level of access some parents believe is their right.

So it will not be unusual to see them strolling around on their way to some office or other.

You might think it would be better if we kept everyone out. But we can't. On the one hand we say we regard schools as open and welcoming places for everyone. On the other hand, teachers and pupils must be allowed to work and learn in a safe and secure environment. But the shadow of Dunblane hangs over us all. No one wants to turn schools into fortresses surrounded by razor wire, so the best alternative is that everyone stays sensible and vigilant.

After all, to conduct learning in an atmosphere of siege and apprehension is not ideal. Schools were never intended to be secure institutions. They are part of their communities and they serve different purposes to different people. Certainly as the emphasis on community education grows, more and more people are coming into secondary schools.

As a result it is becoming very hard for anyone to know who all the adults are on school premises at any one time.

The design of schools too militates against security. Often we work on large and untidy sites with long perimeters. Of course, the bigger the school the more exits are required for safety reasons. And every exit can become an entrance, through carelessness or design.

Schools are not public places to which anyone can have access. Anyone who enters without permission is a trespasser and can be asked to leave.

No one has an unrestricted right of access to school. If you see someone in the building without the necessary pass or if they look suspicious you should ask them if you can help them and then inform someone straightaway if you feel that it is necessary. This is the theme that runs throughout this book. Always act as a responsible adult. A school is full of young people and you must do your best to contribute to their safety.

All children take risks, and vulnerable children take more risks than most. They might do things to win status among their peers who will often make their daily lives difficult. It will be very important for you to be able to talk to your students about the issues that surround them. You need to be fully informed so that you can offer either the advice that they need or indeed know a place where such advice can be found.

You must be aware of what policies you must follow at all times, especially those relating to health and safety. It is also important to note that the security of the students you deal with will be significantly enhanced if you acquire a relevant first aid at work qualification. In this way you can provide instant and informed support.

You may be asked to accompany a teacher and their class on a school visit, designed to extend their learning out of the classroom and into the wider community. It might only be the school car park or a local supermarket but it could indeed be further afield. You will need to ensure that you are fully aware of school policy and of the responsibilities you have. Obviously, you should not be left in sole charge of students unless a proper risk assessment says that it is required and safe. Your role should largely be to assist and report any issues or concerns you might have to the group leader. You might well be preoccupied with one particular student but you cannot ignore your responsibilities if you see other things that make you uncomfortable.

Clearly you must avoid putting yourself at risk of allegations being made about you. This would be a threat to your own security. Teaching assistants can be vulnerable because their job does include a lot of close contact with individual students. For most of us this isn't a problem. We trust those around us and we are professional, and the children are aware of how we are trying to help them. But it is a very fine line between supporting a child who is apparently distressed and becoming a victim of a false allegation. It could happen when you are alone with a student, so always make sure that the door to the room in which you are sitting is open. It could happen in specific situations where you might be offering intimate or discreet care, for example when dealing with incontinence or when you need to restrain a student. You need to be aware and vigilant and ensure that you are complying with school policy.

Of course, it goes without saying that you must never find yourself in physical contact with children, whatever the reason. It is hard to avoid it completely and in all honesty you have to use your own common sense. I have been hugged warmly before now by Louise who had severe learning needs. It would have been heartless indeed to have merely brushed her aside. Of course, Louise had to learn that there were situations when such contact was inappropriate, but you couldn't expect her to know that at the beginning. Together the teaching staff and the teaching assistants worked to improve her social skills and her understanding.

But other forms of contact, such as poking, prodding, pushing and threatening have no place in school. If you cannot interact with children without recourse to such strategies then there is no place for you in schools.

14

The curriculum

The curriculum is the stuff that we teach. That is all that it is. You might think that it is a simple thing but it is not. Because what we want children to learn changes from generation to generation. The things that we once considered important have been replaced by other things as priorities have changed. Information technology is a good example of how a new issue needs to be integrated into the body of knowledge that must be transmitted. But sometimes our society feels that it needs to plan for a changing future and wants to deal with issues that emerge. So the government will instruct schools to teach certain things – the introduction of citizenship is an example of a curriculum change that is designed to shape the future. Things are perceived as needing attention, and then the pressure will be on schools to have an impact.

Look at what has happened to German for example. It was an essential part of the school curriculum but now it is less popular. The language is seen as being less important than others. Spanish is more of a global language and a facility in it can help the economy and is an important holiday skill with consequent employment opportunities. The government is keen to develop the teaching of Mandarin now, in order to prepare us for developing markets and opportunities.

The curriculum therefore is always changing and will be different to that which you experienced in school. Individual schools too can arrange or adjust the curriculum they teach. One school might have an emphasis upon drama either to reflect the way in which they see the school or to reflect the nature of the staff they have. Either way, the curriculum is at the very heart of the school experience.

It has its own language and its own priorities that you will need to learn. There are so many special acronyms – QCA, SATS, DfES, KS3, KS4, Ofsted, GCSE – which you can explore with your mentor. Very quickly, they will become second nature to you. What you will see is that while schools have some freedom, a great deal of what they do is already shaped for them.

Much of the curriculum is set out nationally, outlining to schools the minimum entitlement of knowledge, skills and understanding that should be taught to all students in secondary schools.

The subjects are divided into core subjects which are essential and are followed by all students – like English, maths, science and information technology – and other subjects like geography and history which are non-core. You will also come across Key Skills that link together the different subjects and Basic Skills that underpin all other learning. The National Curriculum itself is organized on the basis of four Key Stages. Key Stage 3 and Key Stage 4 are the ones that are directly relevant to secondary education.

Key Stage 3 covers Years 7–9, which is for 11 to 14 year olds. Key Stage 4 is for 14 to 16 year olds and covers Years 10 and 11. After Year 11 there is a greater variety of provision, with some students staying on in school where it is possible, for more specific and higher-level study, and others moving on to courses at colleges.

What must be taught in any particular subject is outlined in the programme of study. These are the national guidelines that we all must follow. The scheme of work is the means by which the school has decided to deliver the programme of study. It is therefore the case that schools cannot vary the programme but that teaching assistants can make a contribution to developing materials that will be part of the overall scheme of work. Your unique position and the insights that it brings mean that you will be able to ensure that the scheme of work is focused and relevant because it will be constantly reviewed.

The progress of students is measured and assessed by teachers all the time through formal and informal assessments and these are an essential part of their professional responsibilities. Of course, you may be involved in this to some extent as you offer support to your students. You will be making judgements about them and drawing conclusions. To do this in an informed manner, you will need to understand the assessment criteria that the teacher has been using. The teacher should help you with this, and the purpose of this should be to identify the next stage in the learning process. Were the initial concepts acquired? Is there a need for them to be repeated? Is there any way in which they can be simplified?

It also helps to confirm your professional status with the children you support. They will see you as a teacher and you will in such circumstances be behaving as one. You will be involved in the serious business of the classroom. You should never embrace the sort of unstructured work in lessons and around the school that has led some teaching assistants to be referred as 'The Care Bears' in a school I know. You are a professional with a professional drive and responsibilities and that is what you must promote.

Other important concepts that you will come across are 'attainment targets' and 'level descriptions'.

Attainment targets are the concepts and skills that students are expected to have acquired by the end of each Key Stage. You will of course be assisting teachers to make sure these targets are met.

These attainment targets consist of eight level descriptions of increasing difficulty, with the opportunity to recognize performance that exceeds the levels anticipated. Each of these descriptions outlines the performance that students working at that level should be able to demonstrate. This is the basis for making judgements about their performance at any of the Key Stages 1, 2 and 3. Of course, at Key Stage 4 the main vehicle for making these assessments are national qualifications like GCSEs, which dominate the later stages of secondary education.

You can form an impression of the way these level descriptors reveal subtle differences and progression by taking a look at those from a subject of which you have some knowledge. You can then see the way in which teachers have to make fine distinctions between the responses student offer, which can be very difficult in a subject like English where students discriminate between themselves on the basis of how they respond in a complex environment like personal writing.

By the age of seven learners are expected to achieve Level 2, and Level 4 by the age of 11. Levels 5 and 6 should be achieved by the age of 14.

How the learners access the curriculum is a fascinating issue that can become very controversial. Generally speaking all schools group the students together in a variety of ways to enable them to visit different parts of the curriculum. They will often be in a mixed-ability class for their registration period. This means that children of very different abilities will be members of the same group, which meets socially and administratively every day. This is seen as an aid towards inclusion, an important step in breaking down the barriers between students. There will be a number of lessons too where they continue to be grouped in this way – in PE for example. It could also happen in English lessons. It is a very common arrangement especially in Key Stage 3. It means that if you are supporting a child in a mixed-ability setting then you will meet and perhaps have an opportunity to work with students of very different abilities. In other circumstances different arrangements might apply. These mixed-ability groups might be joined together with others and then sets of learners with similar ability extracted to allow different topics and concepts to be explored. This can sometimes happen in subjects like maths.

Some schools prefer to stream the students right from the beginning. They will carry out baseline tests early on in the school year and then arrange them in registration groups on the basis of these results. They will then attend virtually all their lessons in this particular group. This means that students who are struggling to maintain adequate progress are grouped together. Support for a group can therefore be easily targeted and provided. However, it can make under-achieving learners easily identifiable and lead to other issues such as bullying. Consequently you could find yourself working in a number of different circumstances with the same student.

Things change again then at Key Stage 4 when students have more involvement in their learning by making selections about which subjects to study to examination level. Since these groups are drawn together on the basis of student selection, then they can be mixed-ability classes. In other areas of the curriculum, there is a good chance that setting will be introduced, if it hasn't been present before, in order to maximize examination success. Once again, a teaching assistant could be involved in very different situations during the course of a day.

There are different approaches and some work in some settings and not in others. There are so many variables involved and so many different types of teachers, some who are more confident and more effective in one method than they are in another. But in the end it is clear that not all students achieve in the way that we would all like and that we should do what we can to address this.

Obviously, many children, especially those with whom you might often be working, will struggle to make sustained progress in their studies. As a result, there are performance criteria which have been developed which outline attainment for students working below Level 1. You are an integral part of the arrangements that are designed to rectify shortcomings and difficulties. Attention must always be given to a child's individual learning needs – and the work that you do will be instrumental in establishing that they are progressing. You will be part of an intervention that will be established to facilitate genuine improvements.

15

How do children learn?

Fundamentally, children learn by interacting with their environment. It is no more complicated than that. Our responsibility therefore is to provide as rich and stimulating an environment as is possible. In this way, the children's minds will grow and absorb the information, the qualities and the attitudes they need.

If you think about the way you have grown yourself and who it was who played a part in that growth, you can see what it is that schools need to provide. It is a rich environment where learning is structured and supported and which involves different people to support the children – parents, family and teachers.

Your job as a teaching assistant is to be part of that interesting environment that will shape the minds and lives of the next generation. Not every child will have a teaching assistant and those that do and who therefore have a particular need for one should get maximum benefit from that investment. Everyone learns at different rates and in different ways. You are there to try and even out those differences.

A good teaching assistant will become part of that environment. That is what your job represents. You will create opportunities by being an intermediary between students and their environment. You will be providing the structure to help those who find the world of learning a difficult place with which to relate. You are their means and their guide. In recent years a great deal of research has been carried out into learning styles and you need to be as informed as possible about the implications of these developments. It has been shown that we all learn different things in different ways, but that all of us have one particular style of learning that we prefer above others. The four different styles identified refer to visual, auditory, kinesthetic and tactile learning. There will be staff in school who will be able to explain these different categories and help you relate them clearly to the observations you will have made in the classrooms you have visited. It is certainly something that you will need to research.

At a very basic level, you might prefer to see things or to hear about them. You might prefer to move around while absorbing new information. You may learn most efficiently if you can use your hands and manipulate things. Everyone is believed to have a preferred style for learning, and if we can identify it and exploit it we should be able to make the classroom a more successful place.

As a result, it may be that you will feel the need to adapt a particular concept to suit the needs of a learner. A mathematical concept may not be successfully absorbed from the whiteboard but it might be successfully presented by using building blocks or lego. This is fine. This is why you have been employed.

The danger is that a rigid insistence upon the need to accommodate different learning styles becomes far too complicated to manage in the classroom. It is certainly the case that many successful lessons are teacher-led. I have seen a great many lessons like this, and like the classes involved, enjoyed them. The teacher has more knowledge than the young people in the class and it is up to him or her to pass it on, and up to the young people to listen.

There is a huge amount of research into learning styles that those who work in the classroom need to be aware of, although it should not destroy everything that has gone before.

Of course it is true to say I think that students learn things in different ways. A technology lesson and a PE lesson may well facilitate learning in a particular way, whereas the analysis of a poem for GCSE may call upon a completely different approach. But we cannot expand all learning to try and suit concepts of an unchangeable learning style. What we need are flexible learners who may have a style that suits them best but who can adapt. If you learn best when you are moving around or manipulating things, there will be occasions when you will still need to sit down and study the relationship of Romeo and Juliet in some detail. Acting out key scenes may indeed help but there will still be a need for a period of reflection.

One of the ultimate conclusions must be that we cannot, in the daily reality of schools, tune into all the different learning styles in one lesson. Perhaps it is more realistic to expect learners to adapt themselves to the teacher and to judge what they need to do in order to participate and benefit from the lesson. Some learners will need more help with this than others because it is rather a sophisticated skill that we are asking them to acquire, but it does need to be done. It isn't new. Such flexibility has always been required of children in secondary school. It isn't something that we should protect them from either. As they become adults they will need to acquire flexible thought processes and reactions. There is always a time for reflection and consideration.

It is undeniable that some students learn more in one classroom than they do in another and that was almost certainly true of ourselves. It is the relationship between learner and teacher that is the crucial element. There are special teachers that we all remember. We will adapt ourselves to what we do because we like what they do and in that way they help our mind to grow and so change the way they work. This happened because we changed in response

103

to what they did. They didn't change what they did to attempt to accommodate different learners. We responded. There are those who say this is wrong and that we should respond to a student's preferred learning style. But it isn't always practical. What you need to do is to become familiar with the most effective way that your student learns and try to use that knowledge when you need to devise work for them. You might also be in a position to bring learning from different subjects together to form some sort of coherent whole. Making connections could really help and transferring the techniques from one lesson to another could reinforce learning very effectively. It might be a really interesting idea to involve learning objectives from a maths assignment during a PE lesson if the student appears to prefer to learn while moving around. Something like counting or addition or sequencing would be very easy to incorporate.

If you were to ask me what I believe is the truth about how children learn I would say that they learn best in the presence of good skilled teachers who are well supported by appropriate resources and other professionals. Their skills are what will make the difference. Trying to adapt materials to fit into unnatural learning styles will not make the experience any more successful. It is good people in the classroom who will make the real difference. You need to aspire to be one of them.

16

Transitions

A very important part of your work will be to ease students through the transitions from one important phase to another. Some of these transitions will be formal and expected, others will be unplanned events that change lives in an instant. At all these significant moments of their lives they will need support as they make changes. These changes happen to us all and we all have to cope with them as best we can. But those learners with whom you will be working will be less able to deal with some of the changes that happen to them. Without suitable support the whole learning process could become derailed.

One of the clear transitions that brings with it many and varied difficulties happens right at the beginning when students arrive in secondary school. There are those who will thrive and flourish in this new environment. But others will often feel vulnerable and uncertain, especially those who have found school and its work difficult and challenging. This means that it could be a very hard time for the sort of children you support. They will need your help to find a way through the apparent chaos that a secondary school presents to the uninitiated.

In the best planned circumstances you will have met the appropriate teaching assistants from the partner primary schools and they will have passed on to you the important information that you will need if you are picking up responsibility for their learner. And of course, most importantly of all you should have met the learner themselves and been able to offer them reassurance. You need to start building the relationship before they arrive in school, if this is possible. As the adult you need to take the initiative.

You will have the responsibility of guiding them around the school, simplifying instructions, helping them to manage homework demands, managing the different requirements in different classrooms. Your calm and experienced interventions could indeed prove vital. You will be able to judge the success of what you do in the successful integration of the learner into the complexities of the secondary school environment. There will be other changes too within the system that must be negotiated, particularly when the learner moves from Key Stage 3 to Key Stage 4. At this point the student will make a selection about what subjects they would like to study. This is a critical moment in their school career, because they will be determining the shape of their future learning and may indeed set in motion their progress along a particular career path.

They will need support in making their choices during the options process so that they make their selection on a sound basis that points towards a future career, rather than upon some temporary affection or dislike of a teacher. In order to do this they will need plenty of information from yourself and teaching staff, and the careers service, as well as the parents who may well have ideas of their own. It might be that you are best placed to bring all the information together before a decision is reached. Once the courses have started in Year 10 you will need to monitor the initial phase very carefully to ensure that the right decision has been made. You will also be able to ensure that a perspective is maintained and that no minor setback or disagreement is allowed to escalate to the point at which a student decides that they want to change their choice. They must obviously give their new subjects a chance and you can make a real contribution by maintaining a focus on positive things and upon the initial objectives that the student expressed when making their choice. Often what you will find is that attitude and attainment improve among students when they have been involved in making choices about the shape of their curriculum.

During Key Stage 4 the students may also spend some time out of school on work experience or work placement. They can gain an enormous amount from this, yet they can be rather nervous about taking this tentative step into the adult world. Your learner will need to know that they have your support at this time. Because of the close relationship you may have developed, you may well want to be involved in the choice of a placement and its arrangement. You could help compose the initial letters of enquiry and help them prepare for interviews. You can work with the careers service and set up practice interviews which could help to allay nervousness. In some circumstances you might need to accompany them on any preliminary visits. It is very important that those working most closely with the student in the workplace environment are fully informed about any potential issues that might be presented. The workplace is a busy environment and sometimes important health or learning issues can be overlooked. Your student may not have sufficient coordination for example to pour from a kettle safely. They may not be able to work at a computer screen for any length of time. It is always helpful if you can check that these messages have been transmitted to the people who actually need to know the information. To this end it is always helpful if you can visit your student when they are working on their placement. It will offer tremendous reassurance and security for them to know that your concern does not end at the school gate. It will be an essential part of the success of the placement.

Naturally the biggest transition of all can be when they leave school altogether and that relationship between the two of you is formally severed. It might be a natural and expected conclusion but it can be a difficult personal moment. It shouldn't be avoided or ignored. The event may be welcomed or regretted but you must prepare for it. Indeed, you will only have done your job properly if it is a stage that the student has been prepared for over a long period of time. The choices that they have should have been presented properly and an informed decision taken.

Today, it should really be a choice that continues education rather than terminates it. There are increasingly very limited opportunities for worthwhile employment at the age of 16. Unskilled work is increasingly unsustainable. Your students need to seek out the training that will provide particular skills. You might need to support the student in visits and choices, perhaps in a college, as they explore the possibilities. It is another choice about the direction that learning and life will take, just like the one that they made at the end of Key Stage 3. You need to be positive, presenting the advantages of any choices that are made. Positive messages and a positive attitude. There is still so much to learn and it is still fun. They might be apprehensive about a future that does not contain your support but you have to show them that they have the skills and the aptitude to survive and prosper. The sight of a confident young person moving on to the next stage in their education should be confirmation of your professional success.

17

Teaching assistants and health

There are many reasons why you should be promoting healthy lifestyle choices among the students you work with and there are many ways in which you can do it. The most successful way in which you can have a long-term influence is actually by promoting success in education. All the statistics are there that speak of a huge social divide that should give all of us considerable cause for concern.

There is a provable connection between underachievement at school and levels of obesity and heart disease in later life. Some people can overcome such a poor start and turn their lives around but the majority find it very difficult to do so. As a result their lives can remain undeveloped and unfulfilled. Without the proper guidance and education about healthy choices they may remain unaware of what they can do about it. What a waste this can be.

These real issues were recognized some time ago and identified in the National Healthy Schools Programme in 1999. As a consequence schools have to promote personal, social and health education, which includes sex and relationship education and drug education. They must promote healthy eating, physical activity and emotional health. It is a good example of the way the priorities of school are required to change to respond to national priorities. If there is a problem, schools are the best place to sort them out.

It does seem to me that a teaching assistant can play a full role in the strategies that a school might develop. You could run a breakfast club or become involved in sporting activities. Your commitment will be a good example and encourage students to become involved. There are basic health messages that you are well placed to repeat because of your close and fairly constant relationship with students. Reminders about combing hair, keeping clean, brushing teeth, and frequent hand washing may seem rather basic but to many – and there is a good chance they are those you deal with – such messages are not given consistently at home. This can also be the case when delivering healthy eating messages and suggesting a balanced diet based upon fresh produce.

Many of the issues will be covered in Personal Social and Health Education lessons and you will be expected to play a full part in them. These lessons give students an opportunity to reflect on their lives and the world around them. Schools hope that they will learn respect for others and respond positively to the diversity of our society. You might enjoy the lessons very much and you will feel that you are making a genuine contribution in preparing all students for adult life. You will have plenty to offer, because of your different life experiences. These lessons can be fun, but they are not for the faint-hearted, especially when the material gets a little frisky! But you should never put yourself in a position where your embarrassment becomes obvious. Then the focus of the lesson will swing away from the important topic and settle upon you and your discomfort.

Your school should present consistent and informed messages about healthy eating. But it can't just take the form of a set of worthy statements that are then ignored. There must be healthy food on offer to reinforce the messages. This is why a whole-school approach is vital. You and your colleagues must promote these messages to your students, especially the most disadvantaged. You might like to introduce them to new foods, you might like to think about organizing a fruit week for your supported students and others. They would be given an opportunity to try a new piece of fruit every day. You can often get sponsorship for such activities from local supermarkets. You could even involve the students themselves in operating a fruit shop, offering cheap and individual portions at break time. This would certainly build upon the experiences and the promotion of healthy eating that often happens more successfully in primary schools.

It would also help your students if you share your lunchtime or at least part of it with them. This will help you to confirm healthy eating priorities when they come to make their own selections in the dining hall. You will also be in a position to keep parents informed about what is happening to diet when they are not there. They can often be very surprised when they find out exactly what their child is eating at lunchtime!

Physical activity is something you need to encourage among your students. Of course, it is an integral part of the secondary curriculum, but to be honest it isn't always a very popular subject. Underachievers feel humiliated and ridiculed because what they cannot do becomes obvious to everyone around them. They respond by not getting involved at all. This can have long-term health implications for them. So your own encouragement could be vital. Think about setting up competitions among the teaching assistants and their students. You could begin by introducing simple and non-threatening games like throwing a bean bag or by establishing a basketball competition using a ball of paper and a waste paper basket.

Lunchtime clubs have the great advantage of bringing children together from different year groups. Such connections can help a great deal in developing teaching skills and minimizing bullying by establishing new relationships. It will also provide younger students with role models who have had their difficulties and overcome them. It will also give the older ones additional status.

The requirement upon schools to promote emotional health is extremely laudable. What needs to be done is quite long-term but it should involve everyone in the school. Teaching assistants will be part of it all because they will make a contribution – as all adults will – to the emotional climate of the school. This will be achieved through behaviour that will eventually be modelled by the students themselves. Simple actions that show respect, like holding doors open, like forgiveness, like a willingness to listen. This is all part of the way adults create the atmosphere. The way that teachers behave, the way that teaching assistants work together and share and form friendships is a vital example that students should be able to see. The way disagreements are handled and resolved is always a very important example that needs to be set and then commented upon. When we disagree we do not fight. We discuss things. We do not swear or make threats. In my experience, if threats and confrontation by the teachers are common within the school, then they will eventually create exactly that sort of atmosphere among the students themselves. It is through treating our young people reasonably that we will create in them the sort of qualities that we would like them to display.

The willingness to listen when students ask to speak is very important because it creates trust and allows those who are most troubled to find the confidence to express their worries and their fears. But always remember that you might uncover issues that are best left to those with the specialist training. Never be afraid to back off and seek more experienced help if you find your self getting in too deep.

18

To conclude . . .

So, in conclusion, remember, 'Every Child Matters'. It has a central part to play in everything that we do. You need to be familiar with it.

The DfES publication *Every Child Matters: Change for Children* (DfES 1081, 2004) is an important and aspirational document. It identified the five outcomes that children need to achieve as a consequence of their schooling:

- Being healthy
- Staying safe
- Enjoying and achieving
- Making a contribution
- Achieving economic well-being

Clearly this is all very laudable – and certainly all interdependent. They are more likely to enjoy and achieve if they are safe and healthy, for example. These outcomes lie within most of what schools set out to achieve.

But a teaching assistant plays a key role in all this, by helping those who need it most to achieve in a structured and supported environment.

As we have seen, you will be expected:

- To promote healthy choices
- To provide stability in school

- To support learning
- To promote positive behaviour
- To promote achievement

Through the priorities that are established in schools the world can be shaped. No one ever knows what potential lies within a young child, so we must value them all and give them the different types of support that they need so that the future will be a successful and happy one.

Now you might wonder whether it is necessary to say such an obvious thing. Of course every child matters. Surely everyone knows that? But perhaps it is important that such a standpoint is made explicit. We need to celebrate this belief because it reminds us what our job is about. We work in schools, in whatever function we fulfil, to offer opportunities to children. And in the frantic nature of a school community it is easy to forget that there is a wider purpose to what happens in the classroom. It is good to be reminded of it, whether we are a teacher or a teaching assistant.

To summarize your responsibility, it is to promote the concept of self-esteem. Make the students feel good. Show them what they can achieve, that they have a purpose, that they have a role somewhere. You will give them attention and support and they will thus respond.

Every Child Matters provides a common core of skills for everyone who works with children, whatever their role. And like every professional, in whatever field you are working, you need to have an understanding of what you do and why you do it.

So you will encourage the young people you work with to establish full and productive lives, avoiding negative choices and attitudes. You will encourage them to establish positive attitudes towards learning for they will always need to maintain and develop their skills in order to sustain interesting employment. You will above all promote a positive outlook and tolerant and cooperative attitudes. You are helping to build the future.

Everyone has a place where they can succeed and it is the responsibility of schools everywhere to find where that place is and direct the students towards it. Our schools must find the talent and use it for the benefit of everyone in the community. None of us should want students to miss the opportunities that we all in school exist to help them find. Thus schools should be rich and challenging environments, and supportive ones too. For some students, those talents are more hidden, but they are there. You just need to look for them a little harder. When you are working intensely with an individual child you will be in more of a position to identify what they are. They may not have academic potential to fulfil but we all have something within us that means we can make a contribution. And the whole of our society needs you to do this.

The problem is that when the judgement about a school is based upon things like examination results then the pressure is on to ensure that they are good. It becomes the consuming passion of the school. And yet there are some children who can never contribute to these results. This means that they are excluded from an opportunity to be part of these successes. Often these will be the students you will work with most closely. Their achievements must never be marginalized.

It is possible to subject schools to endless criticism, especially in those schools where examination success can be more elusive, but in the end it is the children who go to them who are being criticized. And what this really means is that we are criticizing our own future, creating a negative context in which they are formulating their own experiences. Disparaging what they do, denigrating their achievements. It might be a self-fulfilling prophecy.

We owe it to them to be more supportive and less destructive.

I believe that a good teaching assistant can have an enormous impact upon achievement in school and can transform attitudes and attainment. By coming between students and their work you will be helping them learn new concepts and develop their understanding. You will help your students to learn concepts in a way and at a time when they are ready to do so. And you will release teachers to concentrate upon the highly professional aspects of preparation and assessment for groups of children. You will work with them too, offering support and advice, improving your own knowledge and acquiring new skills. As a result you might decide that you want to join them.

It is a job that you should feel proud of doing. It is entirely worthwhile and enjoyable. You will form close relationships with children and you will take pride in their achievements to which you will have made a genuine contribution. Make it work and it will be the finest achievement of your professional life.

How will you measure your success? You must always try to increase the numbers of young people remaining in full-time education until at least age 18 and to increase the number of students leaving school with functional literacy and numeracy skills. Schools need to provide a balanced and challenging curriculum in order to achieve this, supported by skilled professionals like yourself. That is what your job is designed for. You will judge your success in the long term, not in weeks or terms. In your work you are trying to influence the shape of our future and that isn't achieved overnight. It happens as a result of sustained and informed commitment. You can be proud of having an opportunity to make such a contribution. Use that opportunity wisely.

I hope that you have found this book useful in introducing you to the fascinating complexity of secondary schools and what goes on inside them. It should have given you a sense of where I have spent my working life and also an idea of why I have chosen to stay there all these years. As I look at what I have written I start to reflect upon the fact that there are many things I have omitted. But that is probably right and proper, because what you need to do now is to build up your own impressions of secondary school through your own direct experience as a teaching assistant. Then you will be in a better position than I to write a book such as this for the next generation of people who decide to embrace this rich and varied job.

Index